PRAISE FOR
AND *MAND.*

M000046019

"With passion, commitment to excellence, and awareness of changes in how we must learn to function in a post-pandemic business world, Dr. Graham applies his concept of Techno-Resiliency to the task of exciting the leaders who will guide the world to productive change in how we do business in any context. Whether we continue to work on business from home, or resume pre-pandemic physical configurations for doing our work, this book will inspire leaders to take a resilient stance to managing the tasks ahead. I know it works because I have seen him do it!"

— Dr. Nancy Maynes, Professor, Nipissing University

"Coming from the former head of human resources for a large organization, Dr. Graham's book *Mandate to Be Great* delivers timely research-based strategies, guidance, and the inspiration needed to help today's leaders overcome the many challenges they are now facing in this post-pandemic reality."

— Glenn Zabarelo, Former Head of HR for the
Ontario Northland Railway

"*Mandate to Be Great* is like a personal manifesto for its author, Dr. Rob Graham. Dr. Rob already has a following and an accomplished career, but I have no doubt he will be a name that will be known worldwide over the next few years with his groundbreaking work. In a day and age where technology is shaping every part of our lives and there are so many 'new world' complexities that people and organizations are challenged with as they balance and integrate people, processes and technology, the wisdom of this book is not only timely, but is also critically needed."

— Corey Sigvaldason, HOP Performance Institute

"Dr. Rob Graham's teachings and message, although timeless, are paramount more than ever to today's leaders in all walks of life. Combining knowledge and experience through storytelling and fact-based evidence, he breaks down core leadership principles into practical and relatable terms. This book is a valuable must read for industry leaders. Thank you, Dr. G.!"

— Dan Spence CEO of 360 Goaltending

MANDATE to be GREAT

The 5 Traits of Techno-Resilient People and Organizations

DR. ROB GRAHAM

with Joscelyn Duffy

www.technoresiliency.com

Published by Redwood Publishing, LLC
Orange County, California

First Edition, 2021

ISBN 978-1-952106-78-1 (paperback)
ISBN 978-1-952106-79-8 (e-book)

Library of Congress Cataloguing Number: 2020925907

Table of Contents

A Date with a Mandate: Making IT Happen

In the wake of the coronavirus pandemic, organizational and institutional leaders find themselves navigating an entirely new world—rethinking structures, facing significant financial challenges, and attempting to empower emotionally depleted employees. And they're doing all this while trying to maintain or enhance productivity with a distanced workforce and a greater number of employees working from home than ever before.

Being thrust into operating a technology-driven workplace can expose inequities, such as lack of training, know-how, and resources, leading to rapid overwhelm. While challenging, this shift can also be one that strengthens our learning and collaborative environments. It can lead to the creation of an organizational community where greater levels of inspiration and innovation that were previously not realized are now possible.

How is it that some leaders are able to overcome inequities, personally and professionally, while managing to be productive and contributing members of their workplace and society, while others struggle to move forward? The answer lies in the ability to be Techno-Resilient. Techno-Resiliency means cultivating your capacity for thriving as a technology-enhanced workplace by maximizing existing resources and team efficiencies, while minimizing costs and the complexities of our new world. You can forge ahead to overcome our "lack of"s and cultivate our capacity to thrive. Your ability to thrive, however, is dependent on your finding inspiration and your ability to offer it to others. It is dependent on a leadership team establishing and empowering teams with a Mandate to Be Great.

Techno-Resiliency and having a Mandate to Be Great is the journey I teach. It is also one that I have lived. At the ripe old age of twenty-five, I graduated with my teaching degree and set off into the working world. Three weeks later, I found myself in jail...or rather, I found myself securing my first formal teaching contract at a jail. There, I was assigned the task of teaching inmates.

Many of my friends knew that I was exactly where I belonged: teaching. Though instead of my everyday existence consisting of a leisurely walk through the school doors with lunch bag and apple in hand, my days began with a series of screenings, frisks, and checkpoints before I finally arrived at my dimly lit office in a small storage area located next to a very stale-looking staff room. From the moment of entry onto the jail grounds, all movement from within the facility and between students had to be purposeful and calculated. All movements and decisions were made with the proviso that I ran the risk of being locked in a cellblock with no way out in the event of a lockdown procedure.

I recall telling my sixth-grade physical education teacher, Mr. Holmes, that he had the best job in the world and one day I would be just like him. However, I never imagined that my "one day" would begin behind bars. As a young adult, I was thrust into a high-stress environment, faced with the task of sourcing some extreme levels of resiliency amid the strenuous daily challenges and risks, a highly diverse field of needs among the inmates, differing opinions on the validity of my work, and a lack of resources to meet the many needs.

Add to that the fact that my support system was minimal. Most of the jail guards made it abundantly clear that they were not advocates or supporters of the inmate education program. Many among them did not believe that inmates deserved the luxury of having access to a teacher and educational support.

What many of the guards failed to understand was that our penal system's process was to place people in cells for extended periods of time until they are actually afforded a trial. Many are found not guilty and are released back into the world, forced to find their way forward. With this keen awareness, I had a unique mandate. It was to identify and serve the inmates who did not have a high school diploma and who were sitting idly in a cell, awaiting trial. If I could equip them with the skills and confidence they needed to reenter the world, their chances of success would increase exponentially.

That short three-month contract spurred me into the field of resilience in education—a mandate that continued to grow stronger with every career opportunity that came my way. From jail, I entered a publicly funded grade school, where I was hired as a special education teacher to seventh- and eighth-grade students. There, I was asked to adapt yet again by finding innovative ways to inspire and educate children with diverse special needs, and fulfill one momentous task. One day, four years into my role, I was called to the principal's office. (After being sent to jail, being called to the principal's office seemed like a walk in the park.) I was told that the teacher in charge of the information technology program was set to retire and by virtue of the fact I had been running an after-school computer club with students, our principal believed I would be the ideal person to take over the IT role.

This was twenty-five years ago, at a time when personal computers were not widely accepted. While they had begun to slowly make their way into homes, they had not yet made their way into the school system. Our computer lab was furnished with ICON computers—self-contained, all-in-one machines built by the Ontario Ministry of Education. Our lab housed forty of these beasts, each complete with a trackball for a mouse-like experience. We nicknamed those beasts the "bionic beavers."

I loved everything about computers and technology, though I had no formal training in the field. Accepting the principal's offer would require the revitalization of my skill set and would be a challenge that paralleled what I had faced in jail. Making use of the existing technology and working with a very limited budget required a tremendous amount of creativity, vision, and resourcefulness, and inspiring and selling the teachers on the new platform would require the same. While they may have had less muscle than the squad of jail guards, my teaching colleagues were ferociously firm in their stance on not wanting to change or adapt to new technologies. Add to that the facts that available technologies were not cost-effective, there was little education that informed their use, and technical support was all but nonexistent. Essentially, we had to act as our own IT department, build everything, and rally support from nonbelievers. This was no easy feat in an environment where the impending threat of implementing a digital platform was causing a tremendous amount of trepidation in educators who lacked familiarity with and confidence in using a digital interface.

Upon accepting the role as the school's IT teacher and site manager, I said yes to the momentous challenge, with one provision: that I be allowed to develop one of the first PC-based networked computer labs in our school system. My first step was to achieve complete buy-in from the principal. Our agreement became that I would welcome the challenge of leading the IT department with the understanding that I could not continue to teach kids while using the antiquated ICONs, because they did not provide the children with the skills and experiences they needed to thrive. The only way I would accept the offer was if I could build a PC-based IT program. Whether my colleagues were ready for it or not, we were living in a PC world, and the bionic beaver was rapidly becoming extinct. And so, there I was, in a room full of dinosaurs, determined to carve out an innovative way forward that would spur our school into the late twentieth century.

There was a brief pause before the principal proceeded to ask me how I intended to "make *it* happen." Her words were not intentional, nor did she know in that moment that "Making *IT* (information technology) Happen" would become a career-defining motto for my teaching and future studies. The mountain I had to hurdle reminded me so much of the book my wife, Jen, and I used to read to our girls. In *Something from Nothing*, celebrated children's author, Phoebe Gilman retells the Jewish folktale about a kindhearted and loving grandfather, who, as a fine tailor, made many cherished items for his grandson from his tattered old blanket. Making one of the first networked computer labs in our school district at the onset of my public school teaching career quite literally meant creating something from nothing. The whole notion of making something from nothing has an innate connection to the notion of Techno-Resilience. The resilient spirit that had guided me through so many of my previous life experiences and technological innovations informed my willingness and confidence to take on this groundbreaking adventure…and every one that followed!

After four months of navigating a large and challenging job that many called unrealistic, I had built one of the first PC-based networked computer labs in our school district, with no funding and in just enough time for the fall term. I felt a deep satisfaction in the knowledge that our students would have access to current technologies. The PCs that adorned the lab were not designed to be game stations; they were built to be part of an information technology program and curriculum that would be used to provide students with the requisite skills and focus for learning they needed going forward. What we had created was much more than a technology-driven workspace; it was an innovative education platform.

As I was putting the lab together with my colleague, Trevor, I also researched and developed a unique curriculum specific to the learning needs of our students and the applicable and necessary skills of the day. In essence, I adapted a business model in which the students entered the classroom on day one as prospective entrepreneurs. All of the skills, tasks, and learning they undertook would build toward the apex: a multimedia presentation, using a data projector, delivered to their "business partners" (the other students in the class), selling their concept and brand. Their business partners would need to evaluate the viability of the proposal and the presentation. Everything was done in a networked lab where all work was shared. (This was more than twenty years ago, when cloud computing did not exist, and it was certainly not the norm in a school setting at the time.) These kids were far ahead of their time, being taught to create effective multimedia presentations using guidelines and design principles that many today still have not grasped.

Throughout the life of the project, I faced and found a way around what may have been perceived as impossibilities, or as I like to call them, inequities or "lack of"s. Data projectors were very costly and seemed out of reach for a school with no budget, but I landed us one for free. It was simply a matter of bringing to life my vision for what I dreamed of for my students'. The ownership and sense of accomplishment I felt in having done it on a dime was somehow magnified. It fueled my creativity and desire to push beyond what I had already accomplished. I did not and could not rest on my laurels. What I had was a mandate for greatness, for innovation, and for resilience, and I rallied a team around me to move that mandate forward into a full-blown reality. Today, the phrase "Making *IT Happen*" has great significance in my training, teaching, speaking, writing, and research, and that singular experience provided me with the key rationale for my book, work, and research, which led to the development of the concept of Techno-Resilience.

Following the organizational and personal impacts of the coronavirus pandemic, each and every leader, employee, student, and organization is feeling the call to become more Techno-Resilient, having been thrust into a workplace that is either techno-enhanced or techno-driven in ways that it has never before been. Even some of the world's top technology firms are being forced to navigate having half-to-all of their employees working from home. *Mandate to Be Great* is a book about where you go from here and how you build Techno-Resilience in order to successfully make your way through the challenges you know inevitably lie ahead in this new world in which we all live.

From all of my academic, institutional, and corporate experience, I learned that the underlying factor in all Techno-Resilient organizations is a deep-set, driving professional imperative at the individual and corporate level. It was one of the most remarkable traits I observed in my years of research with thousands of individuals. This imperative is what I've come to call a Mandate to Be Great, and it encompasses a collective drive and openness to want to be better and to do better in the wake of the "lack of"s and challenges we are regularly confronted with at work and in life. These "lack of"s include a lack of finances, training, motivation, technology, information, customers, and/or collaboration.

In his book, *The Moral Imperative Realized*, Michael Fullan observes the following traits in exemplary leaders: "unwavering but respectful; unapologetically forthright but approachable; focused (on the goal and practices to achieve it); sensitive to building capacity, leadership in others; and celebrating success as a collective accomplishment."

While the moral imperative that Fullan observes in leaders contains some of the same characteristics, a Mandate to Be Great is all this and more. It is a sheer, unwavering determination to offer and be the very best one can be—this, in the wake of any "lack of"s (inequities or barriers) one is confronted with. A Mandate to Be Great is contagious by design. It achieves buy-in because it inspires and moves others into innovative action. As a result of our having built the Techno-Resilience program and PC-based networked lab, the local feeder high school that my students would soon attend revamped their information technology and business programs because kids entering the high school were already at a much higher level of understanding. Having a Mandate to Be Great also builds community. It creates connection and collaboration in ways previously unimaginable, because it brings teams together and stretches the bounds of what they believe can be made possible. That said, I would also argue that a vision is never complete. The moment the vision is complete, you have stopped seeing possibility and dedicating yourself to a mandate for greatness. The mandate needs to be a continuous, ever-expanding vision because greatness needs room to breathe and evolve.

When I noticed the emerging trend of the use of digital cameras (again, pre-twenty-first century), I had the vision of securing five digital cameras and creating an after-school camera club that would teach kids proper digital-photography techniques. As I had done while building the PC-networked lab, I connected with someone in the community who was knowledgeable about digital cameras and invited them in to teach. I secured cameras and a piece of special software that allowed students to integrate into visual presentations the photos they took. The digital photography club students were assigned the task of "photo journaling" various school events, uploading the pictures to the 386 computer, and creating a visual montage to share with their peers.

In the hall directly outside my computer lab, where there stood a large bookcase containing dusty old trophies, I had the janitor create a hole in the concrete wall that would allow me to run a cable to a computer monitor. I installed a computer with the required software to empower my computer club kids to display their montages alongside the old trophies. What we'd created together garnered considerable attention. Parents, students, and other educators flocked to see "Mr. Graham's students' digital showcase." The showcase became a source of school pride and a statement piece showing how technological innovation can lead to inspiration for greatness.

Operating with a Mandate to Be Great is about seeking continuous growth, resilience, and innovation. It is enabled and supported by an organization's leadership team and the required exemplary practices, the most notable of which is collaboration. The mandate acts as a very sharp double-edged sword with the ability to cut through organizational challenges and any perceived lack of resources. Those who carry it are capable of offering an organization a tremendous level of security, as they have these protective factors within their boundaries. They are also able to offer their organizations a terrific amount of clarity, vision, and inspiration, knowing they have a big goal on which to collaborate.

In my research, one significant finding was that any such mandate was also partially fueled by one's desire to make those around him great. When this discovery came to light, I could not help but think how cool it would be if I could just bottle what I was witnessing and then provide it to organizations as something they could put in the staffroom's water coolers or coffee machines! The power and potential of that magical elixir was undeniable. This book is intended to accomplish just that for you...albeit, not without the required work and focus on your part.

Whether you are trying to figure out how to do more with (a whole lot) less, seeking a competitive edge, or looking to create a more adaptive workplace, this book is a leader's guide to building Techno-Resilient teams today and tomorrow. It is for organizations that have a desire to be better and to do better, and for those who have or aspire to have a professional imperative for greatness, no matter the challenges, shifts, or "lack of"s they face. Inside this book, you'll find the research-based strategies required to thrive: from sourcing cost-effective solutions and creating sustainable break-throughs for every perceived barrier, to shaping a psychologically responsive working environment and uncovering new efficiencies. This book and work will rekindle your determination to do and be better, and propel your Drive to Thrive to the point of creating a truly Techno-Resilient and Techno-Efficient organization.

Today, you need to have your dispersed workforce of employees guided by a professional imperative, a mandate, with an accompanying skill set that will help guide them and allow them to be more able, willing, independent, and self-sufficient workers. If you believe leadership gurus like Jim Collins and Simon Sinek, then you must believe in your employees. In today's uniquely challenging environment, employees need much more than to be self-motivated in the manner some thought leaders suggest; they require something much more: a driving professional imperative. Without this, it will be merely business as usual. In a world where everything has been shaken, we must quickly be able to adopt and adapt a *business as unusual* mode of thinking and working. Business as usual will simply no longer do.

The aim and the intent of this work is to provide with you the inspiration, insights, and understanding of the new skill set you and your organization will require to "Make *IT* Happen" when it comes to being truly Techno-Resilient and having a guiding *Mandate to Be Great* in your workplace or within your own personal life space. In these pages, you'll find plenty of surprise revelations, and you'll likely surprise yourself with what you can make possible as you learn to overcome perceived barriers to adaptation and growth, rather than being overcome by them. And along the way, you'll grow more Techno-Resilient than ever before.

If you're ready, let's get started!

A Time with No Template

As a business leader, you've been asked to master the art of being able to see and to do many things at every moment. You must be mentally ambidextrous, with the ability to manage the present, learn from the past, and focus enough to pay attention to emerging social and political trends. You need to do this in order to mitigate risks associated with where and how to spend on innovation that will be your organization's future. You do it all because, as we experienced with great force in 2020, there will be times when you won't see a seismic shift coming at you full thrust.

Every organization has come to face challenges for which they did not have a contingency plan. Almost overnight in 2020, business as usual became business as very unusual, very unknown. This is what I call the "new world." It is a post-pandemic, financially reeling reality, where we are all treading murky waters—waters far more turbulent, deeper, and more complex than ever before. It is one in which many organizations, institutions, and communities have been forced, somewhat uncomfortably, into navigating a full technology-enabled workplace experience...potentially with no IT department or coworkers anywhere nearby to support the seismic shift.

You Can't Google This!

The answer to where you go from here after a shift the size of the one everyone experienced in 2020 is not one you will find in a Google search, though there may be much to be learned from the company itself. In 2018, I had the opportunity to visit the Google headquarters in Boston with my family. As my kids will tell you, it was the highlight of our trip. Almost immediately, my girls, who were ten and sixteen at the time, asked what they had to do in order to get to a job there! For a company to have that much impact and influence on two young people who had only just toured the office building made me speculate as to just what that magic elixir was that the Google executives were putting in the water cooler!

Walking through the Google offices, one could make the case that Google executives strived to meet all of the needs outlined in Maslow's hierarchy of needs theory, from basic human needs such as food and water, to an abundance of self-actualization support. There were places for meditation, yoga, and reading. If you simply needed to shoot a round of pool with peers or play a game of pinball to relieve some stress, no problem; they had that too. There were opportunities for social interaction, conversation, and collaboration that afforded employees the opportunity to feel connected and respected. The many on-site *microkitchens* contained every incarnation of protein bar and fruit available, and they were open 24/7, alongside the coffee and espresso bars and a lodge-style cafeteria, where all food was all free. No employee ever had to worry about packing a lunch. And should they need dry cleaning, a haircut, or a massage, those services were available too, right down the hall.

In a compelling *Entrepreneur* magazine interview, world-leadership teacher Simon Sinek stated something I firmly believe in:

When we provide people with a reason to come to work that they care about, they will give us their blood, sweat, and tears. They will give us their discretionary effort and their passion and their best work, not because they have to, but because they want to. When we give people a reason to come to work, people will come together and put their egos aside to find ways to bring our shared vision to life. When we give people a reason to come to work, they will love their job.[1]

It was no secret what was happening at Google. Sinek hit the nail on the head, as did fellow leadership expert, Jim Collins, with their similar ideas—when you put employees first, only then will your customers *feel* like they are number one.

The magical elixir Google developed was brewed by their structuring their workplace in a way that didn't just make people want to go to work, but also never want to leave. And in truth, Google employees never *had* to leave, as they had everything they needed right there! They had places to play, places to eat, and places to sleep. My family and I saw it firsthand. I even had the chance to jam on one of the drum kits in the music room that was available for leaders to play when they needed to decompress or when they simply wanted to get their Led Zeppelin on.

The Google environment allowed for collective motivation and a mandate for something much greater than oneself. The working environment on the grounds provided the opportunity for an emotionally and psychologically charged working environment like

[1] Koji, David. "An Inspiring Discussion With Simon Sinek About Learning Your 'Why'." Entrepreneur, February 14, 2020. https://www.entrepreneur.com/article/284791.

no other I had seen before. For me, there is no better corporate model to spotlight in this chapter than this one, which exemplifies a psychologically responsive workspace. The management team revolutionized the concept and the feel of what coming to work each day is. With all the needs being exceeded at every level of Maslow's hierarchy, there was no way but up for employees! However, this was before the new world of attempting to master Techno-Resilience in an environment of employees and corporate leaders attempting to learn how to master the science of home work while maintaining productivity, engagement, profitability, and overall contentment. In this post-pandemic era, these are the most human of times, ones that must be approached from a very human place. There is a glaring need for a psychologically responsive workspace with a very high level of "careness and awareness"—the ability of leaders and everyone in the organization to elevate their level of care and awareness for themselves, for others and for the organization as a whole in a way that is felt even when workforces are distanced and not operating out of a singular office as they once did.

Seismic Shifts and Sizeable Challenges

No organizational leader is immune to facing sizeable challenges in the mania of our new world, as a stifling economy shutdown has rippled globally and many face financial trials like never before in our lifetime. As employees rapidly shift to working from home, you and your team are also doing your best to master that home work. As you scan the width and depth of your organization, you may find yourself confronted with a long list of "lack of"s in the wake of your new working model. This list may include, and may not be limited to, a lack of finances, funding, clarity, worker motivation, know-how, and customers. Many of these challenges and "lack of"s have painfully boiled to surface or become supersized in the wake of our new world's realities. The sum total of this new world can be described via the teachings of Vijay Govindarajan, the author of *The Three-Box Solution*. Govindarajan suggests that breakthrough business models are based on utilizing the futurist conception of *weak signals*. Weak signals are all around us in the form of consumer spending metrics, business trends, social trends, technology trends, environmental and political issues, and emerging issues. The signals coming from multiple sources are sometimes hard to pick up, and many times, much like your cell phone with a bad data plan, the signal is dropped. In the context of an organization today, you must open yourself to being mindful of and back in alignment with your ability to detect these signals because it is only once the signals are detected that the real work begins. Then, you need to have the in-house capacity to decode and interpret them.

Based on the *not-so-weak* signals, one thing is certain: it will no longer be business as usual. Here's what we know:

- A business will need to master its *home work*…and not the kind we did in grade school, but rather the kind that physically distances teams and workforces.
- Establishing a psychologically responsive work culture with new levels of social awareness and responsiveness to employee needs will be paramount.
- Traditional views and theories of employee motivation should now be placed under a fully focused and high-tech microscope with the power to zoom in on nuances not seen before.
- Employees are still, and need to be considered, an organization's greatest asset.

Confronted with sizeable challenges and fears, the new world in which you have been forced to operate is being defined daily. As we witnessed with the unfolding of the pandemic, the economy, both locally and globally, continued to expand and contract in response to the metrics provided with respect to the number of cases of those with the virus. In addition to this constant tension, we continue to feel the impact of a heightened social consciousness surrounding the nature of policing in our country, with civil unrest and protests having been at the forefront of media headlines, and most certainly, an uncertain economy. Going forward, the impact of these conditions on the human psyche and the mental health of organizational leaders must not be underestimated. In the wake of the unrest and lingering fears that followed the great shakeup of 2020, proactive organizations came to understand the importance of taking immediate measures to become more psychologically and emotionally responsive to the needs of employees. This is what it means to become truly Techno-Resilient. In this new world, inspiration must become the new innovation, as we experience a glaring need for leaders to move their organizations forward like never before, in a *way* like never before.

Utilizing Govindarajan's *weak signals* in a business context is an incremental process that drives new explorations based on an acute sensitivity to and awareness of subtle changes in the broader environment. Those signals being sent today are scrambled, mixed, and are arguably being sent at frequencies that may be undetectable to some businesses. The changes Govindarajan suggests are often barely perceptible. However, paying attention to the *weak signals* in the broader environment allows an organization the ability to go "back to the future." In this regard, a leadership team can use these signals to guide and manage risk with respect to where and how to fund and drive innovations for the future. It really is an adapted real-life business version of the movie *Back to the Future,* whereby we must be constantly "code switching" from past and present, all with a goal of predicting and preparing for an unforeseen future. However, now that we're in the new world, there's no going back, except to revisit important learned lessons from our past that can serve us going forward.

New World, New Thinking

If you believe that out of desperation can come creativity, then you must believe that today, the creative juices are flowing within organizational teams all around the world. From the outside in, the new world for organizations needs to be reconstructed using a totally revised and updated building code that will allow the organizational structure to carry the dramatically increased weight of the world. When you have less to work with, you must maximize your existing use of technological resources and cultivate a capacity for greater team efficiencies. All this must be done with the realization you will have an employee base that is emotionally fragile.

Facing an emotionally depleted workforce that has been feeling isolated while working from home or grappling with national and global chaos, the taken-for-granted notion of being a self-motivated leader or team member is simply not up to the "building code" by which you need to develop your organization going forward! Fundamental to working with this new building code are some necessary understandings that must take place before the shovel can even break ground. One foundational understanding is that if your team members are not inspired, nothing else really matters, and nothing else will happen. We are facing a new world that is simply too big for the focus to be on oneself alone.

Now more than ever you must be willing to invest the time and mental energy required to better understand and thrive in the world in which we all must now operate. The opportunity and the rewards will come to leaders and organizations willing to accept that within these unusual times, we must challenge taken-for-granted notions of doing business. Today, it is not enough to examine the situation before us from the *inside* out; instead, we must work from the *outside* in—with the "in" representing the inspiration that will become your new innovation and your way forward.

Inspiration Fission: One Question Becomes Two

I t has likely never before crossed your mind that having a self-motivated team would *not* be enough to get the job done in your organization. Yet here you are, post-pandemic, attempting to navigate or renegotiate how to motivate and move your team into the same level of productivity and engagement you once knew or had been previously aiming for.

Amid the many challenges you face in today's new world is the need for a totally reimagined understanding of and framework for what motivates your team and how you motivate them. Having distanced workers seated in their new home offices as they attempt to psychologically and emotionally navigate this new world requires you to become an amateur psychologist yourself, because your team or organization no longer works in a purely office-centric environment and is no longer driven by office-centric rules of engagement. Today, self-motivation alone will not spur employees into action, cohesion, or collaboration. The reason lies in the problem with self-motivation itself: it is an egocentrically driven personality and working trait that does not necessarily mean a leader or employee will be willing to collaborate, inspire others, or be a contagion for innovative professional workplace practices. There is no guarantee that someone exemplifying self-motivation will have an accompanying skill set and understanding of how and why to overcome the workplace inequities that have been thrust upon every organization. In the wake of the new world's realities, you need to be so much more.

If we remove "self" from self-motivation, we are left with something exponentially more powerful than self-motivation alone. That something more is the concept of having a research-based professional imperative—a collective corporate or community engagement in a Mandate to Be Great. This the foundation for how we rise through this time for which we have no previous template.

A Hyper-Caffeinated Approach Works Best

In a world where innovation and innovative products are taken for granted, most of us are immune to the human story behind the product. It's easy to forget to find inspiration in the tale behind a product or business. Each morning I begin the day with my Keurig coffee machine in high gear, pumping out eight cups of finely brewed java—black, per my doctor's orders. Some may say I consume more than one's fair share of coffee a day, though my addiction to caffeine pales in comparison to that of Keurig's visionary leader, John Sylvan. If Keurig's management team could now find a way to infuse the sheer determination, perseverance, and resilience it took to bring the Keurig product and brand to market into every cup, the entire business community would be incessantly drinking their brew at whatever cost.

Keurig's company story is nothing short of hyper-caffeinated. As reported on Boston.com on August 7, 2011, Sylvan purportedly checked himself into a hospital due to chest pain and what appeared to be signs of a heart attack. As the story goes, after a perplexing examination, which found no sign of heart or other troubles, the doctor asked Sylvan if he drank coffee. His response quickly solved the mystery and serves to highlight the level of passion required to *make it happen* in business. He was consuming thirty to forty cups per day—the amount he felt was required to discover the perfect brew in capsulated form.

It is reported that for years, John Sylvan and his partner, Peter Dragone, drew no salary, developed prototype after prototype, and were turned away repeatedly by venture capitalists. This, combined with a few business missteps along the way, resulted in two or more steps backward. The researcher in me dug deeper and discovered that maybe the reason for their success is cryptically encoded in the nonintrusive white capital letters of the Keurig logo that greets me every single morning: it represents every drop that went into creating excellence. The story behind the pioneering coffee-brewing company is one of true excellence in resilience and perseverance. The organizational leaders for Keurig fought hard for everything they accomplished and what they have earned. If there is another lesson you can learn from this story of passion, commitment, and determination to overcome the "lack of"s faced within a business, it is that building and leading a successful business takes guts. Today, the opposition and the challenges you face require more of a hyper-caffeinated approach. Your approach to overcoming new challenges and "lack of"s must be fueled by an "off the charts" level of determination along with a high resilience factor, similar to what the Keurig leadership team displayed. However, you need to accomplish this without putting your health at risk, because you are faced with the additional task of trying to motivate and inspire your teams members' imagination and creativity in a post-pandemic era, when many are simply trying to reimagine life itself.

In this new world, the difference between a professional imperative and self-motivation is crucial. Identifying those with a professional imperative and understanding of how to nurture it within your organization in the form of a Mandate to Be Great is the X factor you are looking for as a leader. Guided by such a mandate, you can seek and achieve continuous growth, resilience, and innovation. Your vision will become one that is scripted through a guiding mandate to be and do better. It will be enabled and supported by your organization's leadership team and the required exemplary practices, the most notable of which is collaboration. If you are aiming to create a revitalized, thriving workplace that can handle the weight of this new world, you need everything to be turned *outside in*. With home work being the new normal and the inability to rely on providing employees with everything they need (or the entirety of Maslow's hierarchy, in Google's case), coupled with the urgent need for a psychologically responsive work culture, comes the requirement for inspiration and motivation to be a collective and innovative venture. Even more than that, it must be made an *adventure*.

To reconstruct your organization during this new time, there must be a focus on cultivating and inspiring rejuvenated workplace morale—one that incorporates an accompanying mental framework and skill set that will fully enable and empower workplace Techno-Resiliency and Techno-Efficiency. With inspiration being the innovation in this new world, those who have a Mandate to Be Great become the driving forces in an organization. If you want the ability to thrive in overcoming current and future hurdles instead of being overcome by them, your modern mandate must begin with *the desire to inspire and to be inspired*.

The Two-Way Street of Inspiration

The need to find inspiration (the desire to be inspired) and our ability to offer it to others (the desire to inspire) are vital sources of innovation for all of us, most particularly in these challenging post-pandemic times. Throughout my years of research while getting my master's in education and PhD in e-Research and technology-enhanced learning, as well as my work as an educator, it became clear that in order for inspiration to be a predominant precursor to innovation, it must be a two-way street. You can be an inspired leader, but if your people are not inspired to learn and to work, nothing else matters, and no real growth or change can occur. What distinguishes those with a Mandate to Be Great from those who are self-motivated is an *internal* mandate to do better, to be better, and to make those around them better. In my research, it has become clear that those with a driving professional imperative are also typified as having a willingness to learn that is accompanied by an equal willingness to teach. The leader with a mandate is someone who is distinguished by a desire to inspire and be inspired, to share and care (a "careness and awareness" factor). This is something dramatically different from a much more limited and isolating notion of self-motivation. When "self" is removed from the equation, the opportunity for inspiration to be more easily cross-pollinated within an organization is made possible.

Teaching technology-enhanced teaching and learning in the faculty of education at the grade school and university/college level, I got paid to help mentor and instruct aspiring leaders and teachers. My job was to inspire creative and imaginative uses for technology in the classroom, and every fall, I began each class by asking one simple question: Do you desire to inspire? However, when I began interviewing and observing the leaders I eventually labeled as Techno-Resilient in my research, I discovered that asking this one question is not good enough. The cryptic title of this chapter, "Inspiration Fission: One Question Becomes Two" gives you some insight into how simply inspiring others is not enough, and nor is the desire to be inspired. You must have both. So today, that singular question with which I introduced to over ten thousand students in my classes over the years has now morphed into two equally powerful points for us all to ponder:

1. Do you desire to inspire?
2. Do you desire to be inspired?

As far as principles for the successful operation of an organization go, it is no easy feat to enact what I now call the DTI (desire to inspire) principle in this tumultuous time in which we live. To be that organizational leader who is regularly willing and able to share knowledge and inspire others, you must be continuously open to engaging, to listening, and to allowing yourself to be refueled by others. This takes mental energy—energy that is easily diverted and rapidly drained in this new world. If you do not understand what is required to inspire and be inspired, it can feel easier to simply remain self-motivated and isolated.

Desire to Inspire

Much of my published writing has been based around "cultivating a desire to inspire." In a chapter I wrote for a book few years back, one of the subtitles read, "Thank you, Mr. Martindale." It was the story of a physical education teacher of mine who sent me, all expenses paid, to the Ontario Athletic Leadership Camp as the tenth-grade nominee. After the two-week-long program, I returned to the high school and was presented with my own whistle and a desk situated within the physical education offices alongside my "teacher idols." He told me I was a leader and he would be relying on me to help coach, teach, and mentor some of the ninth-grade students. I started with teaching a ninth-grade tennis class. I have never forgotten the inspiration, confidence, and belief in self that Mr. Martindale unleashed in me at a very young age. It has fueled me ever since.

If your answer to the question, Do you desire to inspire? is *yes* (as it must be for a leader or teacher in any capacity), then you have no choice but to open your mind and your heart to the explorations and discussions that will take place during the course of this book's teachings. In the classroom, I always prefaced this pointed entry into my time together with students by stating, "If at the end of any exploration of presented technologies, you still believe the chalkboard has the ability to engage, motivate, inspire, and enhance learning more than the technologies, then pick up the chalk and go!" The choice is yours: the complacency chalk or the galvanizing potential of a mandate for greatness!

In this new, post-pandemic world, the secret to employee motivation has been stripped away and necessitates rethinking and re-creation. With employees now working from home, how does a company like Google replicate what they had before? How do they motivate their employees? Will employees have the same allegiance to the organization without the on-site quirks and perks? The researcher in me wanted to dig deeper, so I contacted a Google team member working from home in Boston and conducted a Google Meets video session with him. What I discovered during this casual interview most certainly supports the case for having a psychologically responsive workplace.

As a trained researcher, I generally want to enter these conversations with what I call "eyes wide shut." What I mean by this, is that

I begin with some hunches and expectations about what I think I'll uncover; however, I'm not blinded and biased by my own thinking. Truth be told, I did not expect to uncover what I did, and although there is no statistical validity to these findings, there is a weak signal that must not be ignored!

I asked the Google leader, "Will your allegiance to Google be diminished if you can't work in a physical space that provides all of the stimulation, perks, and quirks that it does?"

His response came with little hesitation: "Honestly, you get tired of all the food and perks. What I miss most was the weekly board games and regular social interactions that the environment provided for. Trying to replicate the social aspects of the job online has been a challenge. A bunch of us regularly meet online to play games on a site we like. We do it to try to replicate some of the missed social interactions that took place at work."

Startling to me was that there was no mention of missing the perks and quirks. It was the social interaction and opportunity for workplace connections, inspiration, and—ultimately—collaboration that he was missing most.

The question for you now becomes, As a result of these new-world realities, will your working reality be connected or disconnected from it? The desire to inspire in the new world comes with innovative thinking. For instance, a vital source of inspiration and collaboration at Google could result from creating virtual Share Hubs, which we'll discuss in depth later in this book. In essence, a Share Hub is an organizational technological upgrade that functions as a part of your *intranet,* an internal network accessible only to your organization. It can be customized and designed with input from your team based on your organizational needs. Built on and backed by research provided by Etienne Wenger-Trayner and his concept of communities of practice (CoP), Share Hubs are virtual portals that can provide so much more than just information. They foster strong connections and collaborations. Share Hubs are an adaptation of Wenger-Trayner's. While a Share Hub or CoP fosters strong ties within an organization and advocates breaking down cubicles so information can be shared and can flow more easily and openly across departments, they can also provide a vital source of inspiration to others within an agency. As the Google leader I interviewed mentioned, this was what he was missing and craving. For you to recognize the need for it within your organization and to provide it via a uniquely designed, agency-specific online portal in the form of a Share Hub is the type of leadership and inspiration your team is looking for at this time.

Desire to Be Inspired

As a result of my research and interviews with those I identified as Techno-Resilient, it became clear that inspiration for them was not a one-way street. The second question, Do you desire to be inspired?, was a critical addition to the DTI principle, in response to what I identified in the actions, reactions, and interactions of Techno-Resilient leaders. During my observations of these leaders in action with others, I could see and feel a driving force within the organizational culture that was resulting in higher levels of Techno-Resiliency and Techno-Efficiency. In their daily work practice, those who regularly offered inspiration were also willing recipients of it. One day a leader may be inspiring team members within the organization via a demonstration or a workshop, and the very next day, that same leader is willingly and enthusiastically engaged as a participant in a professional-development session led by another team member. There was an inspiration workflow that had no upstream nor downstream, but was rather markedly *mainstream*. It flowed with equal ferocity *both ways*.

I ask you this point blank: Do you desire to be inspired? Are you willing to open your mind and your heart to a new perspective and some accompanying strategies and skills that can help you better navigate the "lack of"s that you are currently facing, or are sure to face? Do you want to be a better leader and colleague? Do you desire to be more self-directed and self-sufficient at what you do? Do you simply want to learn some new skills and adopt a new attitude that can help guide you through these times, and all time? Do you believe it is better, and it feels better, to do something because it needs to be done, instead of being told to do it? If your answer is *yes* to some or all of the questions above, you have the qualifications and the mind-set required to create and inspire from a Mandate to Be Great. More importantly, you have what it takes to become Techno-Resilient and to lead your organization, team, institution, or community to being Techno-Resilient as well. You have what it takes to become a vital source of the inspiration, the new source of innovation for our society.

However, if you can't honestly answer *yes* to at least one of the questions, it is my guess that that your *no* or *maybe* will be transformed into a *yes* by the time you complete this book. As you read on, you will learn the specific strategies and coping mechanisms that will empower you to overcome the "lack of"s that exist(ed) within your workplace, in order to provide a technology-enabled learning and working experience for your teams, colleagues, and employees that moves everyone to a place of feeling inspired by a shift in cohesion, collaboration, productivity, engagement, and happiness.

Who Drives Who? Who Drives You?

Some people in your organization will naturally inspire more. Some will naturally *inquire* more. And some will naturally *require* more. But together, you must all desire to inspire and to be inspired more... and when you do, good things will happen! You need to know that in the organizations I researched, there was a reciprocal relationship. It became difficult to determine who drove who. When I spoke with the educators within the organizations, they were fueled by the unconditional support they were feeling from their leaders. When I spoke to the leaders, they were inspired by the work of their team members. When I spoke with the clients (the students), they had nothing but praise for the learning culture that had been created. As one student told me, "I don't have to come to school and power down anymore. I get to power up!" She was referring to her *mind,* not just her technology. In your organization, you need your team to be powering up after a prolonged period of being shut down! This trio of forces stoked the organizational metabolism and kept it fueled to a level that provided much of the impetus for inspiring professionals within the organization to make use of technology in a resourceful, engaged, and student-centric manner. What was created was an inspiration vortex that was difficult to not get sucked into. Who drove whom? is an important question; however, the most important question for you right now is, What do I have to do to create a similar inspiration vortex within my own organization?

Today, more than ever, inspiration must be part of a reciprocal relationship. Ironically, you would be very happy to have leaders who desire to inspire others in your organization, as well as others who are self-motivated. But in today's new world, you need so much more within your organization because you are confronted with so much less. The very notion of *self*-motivation risks placing cooperate leaders deeper into their individual silos, when many are already feeling isolated due to their having to work from home. Today, looking at motivation from the outside in, you must conceive of it and develop it as a collective venture. Just like offering inspiration without a willingness to receive it from others is limiting, in both cases, the Mandate to Be Great you and your organization need today will not be fully realized or maximized without the mainstream two-way street of inspiration.

A long-standing biblical proverb tells us that it is better to give than to receive. While this may be true, you need to recognize the importance of receiving. You are entering workspaces and life places on limited reserves of motivation and inspiration, so it is up to your organization to have a plan for how to refuel those with emotionally depleted tanks. It begins by recognizing that every person working within your company has the potential to be a walking, breathing, portable, and self-contained refueling station for others. So, while it is necessary to give, it's clear that today, more than ever, it is equally as important to be open to receiving. Innovation and resilience will only take place if you are living on a two-way street. If all you ever do is *give,* and you are not receiving inspiration in some form from others, your essential ability to give back and perform with a deep-set professional imperative in the workplace will be jeopardized. Understanding the reciprocal nature of this vital relationship is a cornerstone of developing a Mandate to Be Great.

Moving forward in our new world's workplaces and life spaces, inspiration will become the real innovation! Understanding and nurturing the professional imperative will be vital to your organization's success, and it all comes back to a central desire to inspire and to be inspired. Whether it be in a face-to-face working environment or while operating in isolation at home, the need to find inspiration and the ability to offer it to others will be a vital source of innovation!

As stated in the beginning of this chapter, the simple currency of "inspiration" will be the new "innovation" that your organization is going to need to overcome any "lack of"s that may have been magnified by the current situation. Whether you and your leaders remain connected or you become disconnected is largely determined by your willingness to be guided by a Mandate to Be Great, which inherently seeks and cultivates inspiration and innovation.

In order to get the most out of this book and the insights herein, you must begin this work with a sincere *desire to inspire.* While having a desire to inspire is an obvious prerequisite to wanting to move others into action, it will be equally, if not more, important for you to enter this process with an inherent *desire to be inspired!* As 'home'work is fast becoming the new norm in the wake of the pandemic, inspiration and motivation have taken on entirely new meanings. With workers settling into a home workspace, where the boundaries and expectations are blurry, supports are limited, and time is irrelevant, leadership is needed like never before in our time.

The Science of Home Work

When home workers are working with so much less, how can you expect to get more from them now, when you need it most? The working reality of our new world dictates that many organizational employees must now operate from the safety of their homes, though for many, that means operating in isolation. In the year 2020, plexiglass barriers and physical-distancing regulations of six feet were being used to protect us from the coronavirus, while corporate measures to stop the spread of the virus have magnified the challenge of maintaining social and working connections and collaboration, as well as productive efficiencies and employee engagement. The new world has brought about a collision of unprecedented daily work and living conditions, leading to the creation of resistance in the form of economic stressors, fears, political unrest, and anxiety that have the power to psychologically overwhelm your organizational team. What is required is a way to use this *resistance* to strengthen your collective capacity for *resilience.* This is what it means to master the science of home work.

In the wake of this new world's seismic shifts, time has become a factor of nothing. The normal office-centric, nine-to-five workday has been replaced with a blurry, home work experience, where boundaries are drawn in shades of gray and working time is often dictated by the kids' lunch schedule and minute-by-minute demands. What has become most important is not time itself, but what takes place within it...and that is directed by your team's dedication and motivation to move forward the organization and its mission. Now, more than ever, you need the job done in time and at a level that will advance the organization and everyone who is a part of it.

One critical question for you to ask yourself is, *How will some people be able to manage working at home in isolation with a lack of personal resources and face-to-face interactions, especially those without technical proficiency and problem-solving skills?*

Mastering Your Team's Home Work

Not long after the coronavirus outbreak, Facebook CEO Mark Zuckerberg announced, "We're going to be the most forward-leaning company on remote work at our scale." He anticipated that within a very short period of time, half of his entire company would be working remotely, permanently. Reflecting on my interview with the team leader from Google, I recall he also believed that working from home would be long term. Pushed further on the question of why he felt that would be the case, he stated that Google had already invested in each leader working from home by providing a budget for the purchase of an ergonomically structured home-office chair. The signals he was receiving from Google executives suggested he should get comfortable in his new state-of-the-art chair. He, and every one of his colleagues, would have to find a way to make their home *work*. Zuckerberg has expressed concerns that many other organizational leaders have echoed. In a May 2020 *New York Times* piece that was written shortly after the pandemic had become very real, he voiced apprehension about the level of productivity falling off as a result of having a home-based workforce.

It is faulty to assume that the skills that are required to work with others in an office environment are the same as those needed to work in isolation from home. At the office, information was just two cubicles or one knock away while from home, it's three emails, two texts, and a one-hour Zoom session (or in Mark Zuckerberg's world, one Messenger Rooms session) away!

Responding to very strong signals, the science of home work awakened with the seismic shift of 2020 must be presented to you as a call to action and reaction:

- Your team needs to *come* together when you can't *be* together.
- Your team needs a new understanding of job-specification standards for employees who work from home.
- You can't leave your HR team scratching their heads.
- Your team needs to provide workers with the required training, skill set, and mental framework to work in social isolation.
- Your team needs to challenge what many are simply taking for granted.
- Your team needs to know why "know where" is better than "no how."
- You must know how and when to coordinate, cooperate, and collaborate.
- Your team needs a detailed professional skill set and mental framework for successful completion of home work.

Paradoxically, in a business world that is trying to make up for lost revenue and time, nearly all organizational leaders have a home-based workforce with much less supervision, support, and motivation—and they are delivering less at a time when more is demanded and necessitated! Simply put, you are getting less with less, when what you need is to learn how to do *more* with less.

It is no secret that tech companies like Google and Facebook value the face-to-face working environment and the collaboration and innovation that it affords. As I noted previously, Google incentivized the on-site experience, and so has Facebook. Both companies have done their best to make sure that once their team members have arrived at work, they never have or want to leave it. At the Facebook headquarters, one can enjoy a stress-free shuttle-ride service to and from work, free cafeteria service, and on-site dry cleaning. Much like at the Google headquarters, the goal is (was) to provide a high level of extrinsic motivation for the employee base working from a centrally located office space.

Moving the extrinsic motivation supplied in day-to-day amenities that are provided to something more intrinsically driven has to be the long-term objective for you. However, the new-world order that dictates the need for home work will challenge all of your taken-for-granted notions of an office-centric working culture. In an exploratory research paper titled, "An exploration of the psychological factors affecting remote e-worker's job effectiveness, well-being, and work-life balance," authors Christine A. Grant, Louise M. Wallace, and Peter C. Spurgeon signal a higher need for trust combined with clearly communicated joint goals and objectives specific to home-based work.[2] Also highlighted within this paper is the

---

[2] Grant, Christine A., Louise M. Wallace, and Peter C. Spurgeon. "An Exploration of the Psychological Factors Affecting Remote e-Worker's Job Effectiveness, Well-Being and Work-Life Balance." EconBiz, January 1, 1970. https://www.econbiz.de/Record/an-exploration-of-the-psychological-factors-affecting-remote-e-worker-s-job-effectiveness-well-being-and-work-life-balance-grant-christine/10010166318.

need for well-established boundaries and specialized training for those who are working from home. That said, it is you, the leader, who is spotlighted in this research. It is stated that all leaders must provide a high level of emotional and training support for home-based workers.

It could be very easy to let this new working arrangement impede the genuine need for human interaction and what you are able to create as an organization, especially without a template of how to navigate and master the science of home work. The aforementioned research team offered a wake-up call in that they found little evidence of training being offered to home-based workers. In fact, many managers may not be fully cognizant of the need for remote workers to become competent in this new domain so they can fully benefit from this newly mandated style of work. Mastering the science of home work requires new thinking and new methodologies than those you have used in days past. Where social distancing and isolation offer great protection on a personal level, in the business world, isolation from others has the opposite effect. It starves creativity, collaboration, and inspiration—the very things that need to spread in order to foster growth and innovation.

Offering your team training for the sake of training accomplishes nothing. Always beware of bells-and-whistles professional development (PD). This type of PD is characterized by a lack of depth and breadth in terms of what is offered, is generally presenter-centric, and leaves the participant feeling it was wasted time. It also most often does not take into account the needs of changing times. You can no longer afford to waste time when you are trying to make up for what has already been lost in the flux of recent seismic shifts. The question you must ask yourself is, What has changed with the office moving to home, and what is needed to support the move in a manner that does not degrade productivity and worker engagement?

Where the Solution and Science Start

Part of the solution needed to master the science of home work lies in developing a psychologically responsive home-based workspace where boundaries are set, along with clear expectations. Here's the catch: setting boundaries alone undermines the need for your team to be intrinsically motivated, coupled with the requirement for a reimagined skill set, along with developing a pseudo form of face-to-face collaboration many tech companies have long believed is necessary for innovation and inspiration. Achieving full balance and results can be a daunting task, but with a clear plan, it can be accomplished! As I will reveal in later chapters, the concept of intrinsic motivation that is commonly referenced is intertwined with my notion of the professional imperative, or "Mandate to Be Great." The mandate goes far beyond self-determination and becomes a driving force in an agency. What you need to know is that cultivating the mandate for greatness within your organization of home-based workers takes place when you establish the conditions for your team to feel competent and valued in what they do. When you begin to harness the value that comes from the collective mind, and you get others to place the "self" on the shelf and strive to master the science of home work, you embark on a very exciting collective journey of continuously striving for excellence with your team.

The Psychologically Responsive Workplace

There will be some of you entering this new working landscape with the required deep-set professional imperative in place, being able to guide your team in getting their home work done with little support. However, many of you are just coping, and coping is not enough.

Given the great personal and global challenges of 2020, building a psychologically responsive workplace is critical to mastering the science of home work. Techno-Resiliency is highlighted by a strong desire and a willingness to overcome some of the noted "lack of"s in a bid to make technology (home work) work in a way that helps you and your organization, institution, or community thrive going forward.

Taking some creative liberties with an old adage: out of desperation must come leadership, now is your time. Mark Zuckerberg's statement that he intends to lead his company into the new realm of home work by establishing protocols and recognizing the need for home workers is sending a powerful and proactive message to his team: he intends to lead and not follow. Having frequently come under fire for his leadership and decision-making abilities, he realizes this is not the time to flounder—and so should you.

Many times in my storied life I have seen and lived the adage, "Adversity breeds creativity." However, the precursor to a creative and innovative endeavor must be *imagination.* In a course called "Imagination, Creativity in Education," which I codeveloped as a university professor, many were perplexed that it was not called "Imagination <u>and</u> Creativity." The fact is, you have to see it, conceptualize it, imagine it, and believe it before the creative process can take over—imagination *then* creativity. Mark Zuckerberg's driving mandate to do better and be better via his actions, reactions, and interactions will likely drive the required innovation that needs to occur in his organization. He is prepared to overcome as opposed to *being overcome* by the moment. This is to say that it is essential you understand what a deep-seated and intrinsic professional imperative (Mandate to Be Great) is and what you need to do to enable it. It drives your organizational team to "just do it" and "do it with integrity" in the face of adversity.

Another research-based concept that requires understanding in the name of shaping a psychologically responsive workplace is self-determination. Pioneered by psychologists Edward Deci and Richard M. Ryan, the Self-Determination Theory (SDT) of motivation was outlined in their 1985 book, *Intrinsic Motivation and Self-Determination in Human Behavior*. In the work, the authors highlight the need for people to feel a sense of growth, as it was their finding that challenges and taking in new experiences are essential for personal fulfillment. In essence, people in the workplace can begin to become self-determined when that workplace provides an environment in which an individual can feel a sense of competence, relatedness, autonomy in what they do. As I will reveal later, the problem with self-determination in today's organizations is that in the workplace, the self must now be subservient to the power found in the collective and the collaborative spirit. Focusing on the latter is how you thrive and master the science of home work, because it offers the opportunity for forging a deep-set and driving mandate for greatness. As we saw earlier, such a mandate is that which pushes an individual to do better, be better, and make others around him or her better. It could be said the mandate is self-determination on steroids!

In a 2005 review of research on what motivates workers, titled "Work Motivation: Directing, Energizing, and Maintaining Effort," psychologists Adam M. Grant and Jihae Shin dig deep into the work-related processes that direct, energize, and maintain action toward a specific job or project. Carefully unpeeling and critiquing many theories related to motivation in the workplace, they get to the core of the matter with Self-Determination Theory. As they note, according to the theory, workers have three main psychological needs that, once met within the organization, can lead to worker motivation becoming intrinsic, which can be transformational for your organization. The three needs are as follows:

1. Autonomy
2. Competence
3. Relatedness

Here's a breakdown of each: Autonomy is the feeling of having choice and discretion. Competence is the feeling of being capable and effective. And relatedness is the feeling of connectedness to and belonging with others. When you are able to foster an organizational culture that allows your team to have these needs met, you will have the fertile ground required for a Mandate to Be Great to truly take root. Only then can it become something intrinsically motivated that grows deep into the soul of your organization and people. In my research and work with those I labeled Techno-Resilient, I uncovered all of these needs being met by the organizational structure, and the result was obvious in the actions, reactions, and interactions of the workers.

By applying the self-determination principle, you will further realize just how important building a psychologically responsive workplace is, how it connects to the professional imperative, and just how in control of structuring it within your organization—through your leadership and actions—you really are. But, just like you need to replace the concept of self-motivation with a mandate for your organization by seeing it and enacting it as something collective, self-determination is also limited by the focus on self and must be brought into a collective capacity to help you truly thrive and realize resilience in this new world. Giving your organizational team a template to work from in the form of a Techno-Resiliency skill set (which you will discover in the 5 Traits chapters) and a Mandate to Great shows your organizational team you are determined to give them all of the essential elements they need to become self-determined, recognizing your goal is for a collective form of determination. For this to happen, you will need to expand the pockets of resilience that exist within your organization.

Keep It on the Rails, and Nobody Fails

Given the dueling needs for isolation for protection from a pandemic and face-to-face interaction with colleagues at work, you and everyone on your team are faced with the reality of needing to find a way to regularly check your conceptual baggage at the office door. And for those working from home, that may be the bedroom door! You will need to be guided by something far greater than the sum of the fears created by daily life stressors and those caused by the ongoing economic and political chaos that has enveloped us.

For you and your organizational team, the new world can be likened to taking a ride on an emotional roller coaster. Up and down, around, and in between, you are navigating two juxtaposed working and living realities and the impact of isolation. The science of home work is about maintaining the smooth operation of this roller coaster so no one (and no system or process) goes off the rails and everyone can still enjoy the ride. Along the way, mastering this science will mean that you'll meet resistance. You'll need to develop your resilience muscle.

The struggle and the pain we're facing is very real for individuals and organizations alike. We have been hit hard financially and emotionally, and for those with a resilience muscle that is underdeveloped, flexing it can be difficult and painful. Everything that the world witnessed in 2020 has had a trickle-down effect, and the result is the need for a new, reenergized skill set and a heightened level of trust between workers and the business that will be fundamental to an organization's successful operation. With no boss hovering over the workers' shoulders and no visible managers or supervisors in physical sight to keep a finger on the pulse, self-determination, initiative, and problem-solving skills, a deeper-set mandate for greatness to get the job done from home will be required to thrive and maintain productivity going forward. This mandate will give you what it takes to be truly resilient, even in the face of unprecedented resistance.

Make It Like a Military Mission

From my role on the board of directors for our local Military Family Resource Centre (MFRC) and as chair of the human resources committee, I learned that providing a psychologically responsive workplace is more than just a far-fetched idea on the military's radar screen. As a leader you have an ongoing mission in place to ensure a psychologically responsive workplace is fully developed and sustained. As a board member, the process for our organization began with me offering a presentation to all board designates, ensuring that, as leaders and governors within the organization, we would lead by example and remain aware of the emerging needs of our employee base and the social and political trends that push us. As chair of the HR committee, I took the lead as policy developer and overseer by ensuring the language within our policy contained a "careness and awareness" factor.

There is a financial and an emotional cost for *not* providing a psychologically responsive organization. It comes with a greater risk of workplace conflict, grievances, turnover, disability, absenteeism, and low employee morale. In a world where nearly every business leader is facing risky business, why risk anything further, especially the emotional health and safety of those in your organization?

Remember, two of the biggest authorities today on leadership, Jim Collins and Simon Sinek, both implore organizations to build the organization from their leadership team *outward*. The greatest question surrounding the mastery of the science of home work boils down to how you will support this new working world from a very human perspective.

According to the April 27, 2020, analysis titled "Mitigating the wider health effects of COVID-19 pandemic response," international health experts Margaret Douglas, Srinivasa Vittal Katikireddi, Martin Taulbut, Martin McKee, and Gerry McCartney report that the impact of social distancing poses a multitude of potential health effects. Some areas that could be impacted include the following: loss of income, the effects of prolonged social isolation, disruption to essential services, health-related behaviors (including the potential for substance abuse and online gambling), disruption of education, psychosocial impacts (including anxiety), and the suffering of family relationships (including increased domestic abuse). Recognizing and understanding these effects means that you will need your human resources team to immediately put your policies under a microscope set to full zoom in order to realize your true post-pandemic magnification power. Look to ensure that your existing policies reflect the understanding and awareness of the long-term, wide-ranging health and emotional effects of the COVID-19 pandemic. Providing your team with clear, regular supportive communication is a starting point. Backing it up with policies that recognize, alleviate, and mitigate the impacts being felt by your team in the wake of the pandemic will aid in cultivating a collective "we care" spirit that is the essential driving value in those with a professional imperative.

The effects listed above can act as starting points for your HR team's investigation and for building the psychologically responsive workplace required to master the science of home work. With this in mind, look to ensure your policies are not only psychologically responsive and proactive, but also have an awareness of, and supportive measures in place for, the areas that may be negatively affected. These include the following:

- Family relationships (abuse and violence that may be caused by home confinement)
- Economic effects (income loss, stress of falling behind or trying to catch up on payments)
- Health-related behaviors (reduction in physical exercise and/or potential for increased alcohol consumption, drug abuse, online gambling, etc.)
- Psychosocial impacts (anxiety, fear)
- Traffic/transportation (restricted public transport resulting in reduced access for people without a car)
- Education (children being home schooled or dealing with online learning)

Your leadership and HR team will not be judging you by your policy manual, but rather, by your daily actions and reactions to their needs. Be the example. To guide your actions going forward to help shape the action, reactions, and interactions your organizational team has in response to the challenges of this new world, consider the following critical questions:

- Does your current work culture have in place protocols that enable a psychologically responsive workplace?
- Are you confident the same level of innovation and productivity can be achieved with leaders working from home?

- What will your human resources department be looking for and creating in terms of a job mandate and specific skill set for home-based workers?
- Do you have in place a Mandate to Be Great? If not, how can you and your team members come together to begin shaping and implementing one?

In a paper commissioned by the Mental Health Commission of Canada (reaffirmed in 2018) titled, "Psychological health and safety in the workplace: Prevention, promotion, and guidance to staged implementation," the facts presented are hard for a leader to turn away from…and that was pre-pandemic! Looking at the paper today through a post-pandemic viewfinder, I find that there is a far greater sense of urgency around the suggested strategies and policies. The paper contains a 'what's in it for me' list that presents you with a compelling case for implementation of all policies that support the development of a psychologically responsive workplace that makes home work! They can be summed up as the following:

1. Organizational excellence
2. Cost-effectiveness
3. Recruitment and retention
4. Risk mitigation

As stated directly in the paper, "Workplaces with a positive approach to psychological health and safety are better able to recruit and retain talent, have improved employee engagement, enhanced productivity, are more creative and innovative, and have higher profit levels. Other positive impacts include a reduction of several key workplace issues, including the risk of conflict, grievances, turnover, disability, injury rates, absenteeism, and performance and morale problems."

Given these facts and the post-pandemic reality, the provision of a psychologically responsive workplace is not simply a perk; it is a must-have. In providing the supports that lead to these outcomes, you automatically lead. The good news is that in a world where so much is blurred by fear and obscured by uncertainty, the process for ensuring you have what it takes to provide a psychologically supportive workplace is not out of reach. It is largely dictated by the questions, How bad do you want it? *and* How much do you value it?

In the 2010 research study by Maureen F. Dollard and Arnold B. Bakker, titled, "Psychosocial safety climate as a precursor to conducive work environments, psychological health problems, and employee engagement," the authors note that organizational responses and commitment to the development of a psychologically responsive workplace is scattershot. Importantly, this study was written in 2010, pre-pandemic. When reading this type of research today, you simply add exclamation marks after everything you do going forward! These scholars point the finger directly at leadership and senior managers, and advise you must be involved in the process of enacting policies, practices, and procedures that promote a psychologically responsive workspace. They go so far as to state that it is a social, moral, and legal imperative for you to do so. In a post-pandemic reality where the psychosocial issues your team is dealing with are heightened, you must also rise to meet the challenge.

In the context of the Mandate to Be Great that must develop to create a truly Techno-Resilient organization, providing a psychologically responsive workspace is part of the extrinsic fuel source that fires the professional imperative. Having established boundaries, practices, procedures, and supports that can enable and activate a psychologically responsive work culture empowers your team to operate with some assurances. It mentally frees everyone up within the organization. The result will be enhanced worker engagement and productivity.

Letting your team know you have a high "careness and awareness" standard within your organization will pay dividends. Within the science of home work, it provides your team some of what is lost from the quirks and perks of an office-centric workspace. Instead, those quirks and perks should now be found within the policies and practices that offer them a comfort level similar to that which they would have on a coffee break in the newly renovated office lounge.

You have read this far, and you know the way. It starts with *you*. You lead by leading with a mandate for greatness. Either you inspire and elicit intrinsic motivation within your organization as an inspirational team leader, or if you're in the position to do so, you advise your HR department to react, inspire, and support with a psychologically responsive policy that empowers the professional imperative. With a guiding Mandate to Great, your HR team can refocus, restructure, and revitalize policies and interactions.

In a post-pandemic era, we all need to master our home work in order to get the job done right. As you continue to discover, the Mandate to Be Great is about offering your team something that meets the resistance you are facing post-pandemic. You'll learn to develop a powerful counterforce in the form of a collective and intrinsically fuelled desire and ability to do more with less, to do better, be better, and make those around you better. Consider it a lifelong business trip you and your team must prepare for by first unpacking your organization's pre-pandemic conceptual baggage, and then repacking it with the guidance you take from the rejuvenated and inspiration-charged mandate for greatness.

The great news is that establishing a psychologically responsive workplace is not a totally altruistic endeavor. In this post-pandemic era where you are required to do more with less, there is something in it for you. Providing a workspace where the professional imperative is supported and nurtured will be your greatest reward. Make no mistake about that. However, the research commissioned by the Mental Health Commission of Canada is clear-cut. Agencies with an affirmative approach to psychological health and safety see benefits in recruitment, retention, employee engagement, productivity, innovation, and profit levels. There is much to be gained.

Move Over, Forrest Gump; Enter the Resilience Junkie

Every great leader understands that in these most human of times, the employees, the people, must come first. True mastery of a psychologically responsive and productive workplace that has mastered the science of home work during these modern times comes in the form of resilience. Resilience means having both the mental framework *and* skill set to navigate a time for which there is no template.

In a world where we are facing a global pandemic, a crippling financial crisis, and protests of record size, our ability to be resilient and build resilience is being tested in a way that many of us have not known in our lifetime. In the wake of everything that has happened and is still happening around us, it could be said there is not one person alive today who has not been resilient, as we are all finding our way through it! A simple dictionary-based definition of resiliency refers to an ability to "bounce back after problems." The research on resilience, however, goes much deeper. As a graduate student in the field of child development, I was exposed to the theory of resilience at a time when it was just emerging in popularity. I was fascinated by this theory, which was grounded in psychology with roots in other disciplines, including sociology. The theory of resilience and vulnerability captured my attention because it had as its foundation an inherent optimism and a desire to learn from individual case studies of those who had overcome extremely challenging life situations and those who had adapted in a positive way.

The original resilience research was pioneered by Norman Garmezy, as he revealed processes that seemed to protect and propel students toward growth and adaptation. In 1991, Garmezy and Ann Masten released a research paper that defined resiliency as a "process of, or capacity for, or the outcome of successful adaptation despite challenging and threatening circumstances." Resilience research provides a compelling reason to move beyond examining risks and deficits. Garmezy focused his research lens on understanding the "protective factors" that could be taught to children existing in challenging social environments. He believed resiliency was something that *could and should be taught.*

In her 1999 paper, "The Foundation of the resiliency framework: From research to practice," University of Berkley, California, scholar Bonnie Benard cautions that resilience research demonstrates that the practice is a dynamic process and not just a program.[3] A focus of developing resilience must clearly be on the optimism and hope it affords, not the risk factors and challenges it is built to overcome. This means that moving from a limited focus on risk and barriers to one of something grander grounds your team's work and your professional practices in a foundation of optimism and inspiration. As we explored in the chapter titled "Inspiration Fission," these two factors

---

[3] Community Bicycle Center Follow. "Resilience Bonnie Bernard." SlideShare, July 29, 2013. https://www.slideshare.net/cbcad2010/resilience-bonnie-bernard.

are also essential ingredients for building a mandate for greatness in your people and within your organization.

Facebook COO Sheryl Sandberg provides us with a sensitivity check all leaders can benefit from when it comes to building resilience within your people. In her 2017 book, *Option B,* Sandberg joins esteemed Wharton psychology professor Adam M. Grant in taking the reader on the most emotional of journeys as Sandberg pours her heart and soul into sharing about living her life after suddenly losing her husband. In Sandberg's story, it's clear that no online community or amount of money or success—not even the deep-set and driving Mandate to Be Great that I implore you to inspire within your organization—can inoculate one from the pain of grief. In the book, Sandberg offers leaders an authentic appraisal of the need for a workspace that facilitates open, sincere, and raw conversations that really are the underbelly of the organizational beast. Daily interactions must take place with a heightened sensitivity to the human condition. Regular courageous conversations in which you and your team own your failures and learn from your successes must be an inherent aspect of the psychologically responsive workspace. They will allow you to master the science of home work and build your capacity for organizational resilience. Anything less is less than should be expected, and anything less will stymie progress. You need to have two "Plan A"s.

What was most compelling for me as I read *Option B* in the post-pandemic era was Sandberg's heartfelt revelation that "We are all living with option B…How do we make the most of it?" There is a portentousness in this statement, as well as an intimate connection in her story and revelations, along with the need that every leader faces today for a psychologically responsive and aware working space. There are intended and unintended lessons that can be learned from Sandberg for business organizations that today are forced into living with Option B, or perhaps for some, just barely surviving with Option C. Every single one of us must build our resilience muscles because we will all come to face a time with no template, just as Sandberg did on a deeply personal level.

Move Over, Forrest Gump

Looking back at a very early age and stage of my career, even before any of my formal education, I realize that my ability to be resilient was critical. Teaching at the jail, I was regularly faced with different forms of adversity. I constantly had to find ways to overcome a lack of available resources, and as a new teacher in a very unconventional role, I had received no formal training on how to teach in a penal institution. Every day, while entering the jail and beginning the rigorous screening process, I had to overcome a lack of confidence and training...and that was just getting into the workplace.

Later in my career, while taking on the pioneering task of building one of the first networked computer labs in aa junior high school, I was faced with overcoming a lack of knowledge about what to do and how to do it. With no budget and no available computers in place, I had to face adversity in the form of trying to make something out of nothing. Although I did not know it then, the seeds for Techno-Resiliency had been planted, and those seeds and the notion of Techno-Resiliency were sowed in exotic and faraway places early on in my career. They were rooted on the Big Island of Hawaii and then in a small town on the outskirts of Sapporo city on the island of Hokkaido, Japan. These Forrest Gump–like adventures were all a part of my passion for "chasing the experience," and they were elevated by my desire to excel in the midst of humble surroundings and with the lack of resources and skills I regularly faced.

After having gotten kicked out of the house after high school, I was offered the opportunity to attend the Royal Military College of Canada to study engineering and play hockey. Hockey was my passion; engineering was not. Instead, I opted to join the army as a gunner in artillery, in search of something to test my physical and mental limitations. I entered in the best condition of my life and crushed everything thrown my way. The result was my being nominated a top recruit and being offered an opportunity to become part of a special forces squad of paratroopers. I quickly discovered the hard-drinking and Friday-night barroom-brawl lifestyle was not for me, and so off to Hawaii I went to teach!

The year was 1987, and I was twenty-one years old. I set off for the Big Island of Hawaii and the town of Kailua-Kona to teach physical education at a small private school. While there, I taught children from all over the world, instructing them on a small outdoor basketball court, with very limited equipment and resources. One day, I was desperate for resources and asked the principal if I could dig around the school grounds to see what I could find. She was grateful for my offer to rummage around and attempt to put some order to the cluttered storage areas. In my quest, I found what I jokingly referred to as "Canadian gold," a full set of floor hockey sticks! For the next few weeks, I taught children from Africa, Germany, England, California, Hawaii, and the Philippines how to play floor hockey. Many of the other teachers and students would come out to watch the action as I officiated the games in true NHL fashion, complete with a penalty box that kids loved being placed in! The point of this story is that in order for us to thrive, determination, resourcefulness, and creativity were required to make up for the "lack of"s and to build resilience. While in Hawaii, I continually worked to overcome a lack of experience, a lack of formal training in the field, and a lack of resources so I could do the best possible job for my students. I was forced to lean on my ability to be resilient. However, the resilience I required to live, teach, and work in this environment needed to "Biggie-sized" when I accepted a new challenge six months later upon being invited to teach on the island of Hokkaido in Japan.

I landed in Japan with forty US dollars in my pocket and a picture of the gentleman who was supposed to pick me up. All I had to go on was a verbal agreement to teach conversational English at a small church in exchange for room and board. I would be lying if I tried to romanticize my first few weeks in the city of Sapporo. I arrived after a fourteen-hour flight, jet-lagged, disoriented, and second-guessing every aspect of my decision to leave Hawaii. I had landed in northern Japan during the height of wintertime, wearing summer clothing. It was the late '80s, and foreigners were few in Japan, especially suntanned blond guys! Add to that the issue of the language barrier and a culture that was so very different from all I had known, and the stage was set for further resilience building.

When I arrived at a large hall on Hokkaido, there before me, on the stage, sat a drum kit. The family I stayed with ran a small church, and the father was a musician who loved to entertain others with his guitar. On that first night, it was determined that I would be part of the entertainment. Having not played the drums in years and having never heard any of their songs, combined with the fact everything was communicated in Japanese, I was extremely anxious. I recall looking out from behind the curtain before the show and seeing a huge audience. It felt like a very bad dream. I considered faking sick, and to this day, I don't recall what I played or if I even played at all. All I remember is sitting in front of a few hundred Japanese citizens who I felt were all fixated on this foreigner who had absolutely no idea what the hell he was doing.

During my time in Japan, I taught conversational English to

young children who did not speak English. I was forced to rely on instinct, creativity, and determination. While I worked for my room and board and to help the young family I was living with sustain their church, I was afforded a way to earn some spending money. Each week, I visited a local school and conducted workshops with each class. I went from class to class, providing mini-lessons in English. Many of the school's teachers and students had never seen or heard a *gaijin* (a non-Asian foreigner) before. I would often call children up to the front of the room to dress up in my "oversized" clothing and conduct an English lesson based on this novel experience. It was always a hit! Between the language barrier and lack of resources, we did not have a lot to work with, but we always made it work. At the end of each of my classroom visits, the entire school would assemble so teachers and students could ask me questions through an interpreter. I would be presented, in a very formal ceremony of sorts, with a "gift" that was often a wonderful trinket. Importantly for me, there was also a monetary gift that allowed me to purchase a few goods when needed.

Based on both my research and life experience from a very young age, I have determined that there is a certain fascination with the spirit of resilience, where it comes from, and how is it sustained. The feelings of accomplishment you get when you have done something in the wake of adversity are somehow heightened. It may be that one reason people who are considered to be consistently resilient is that once they experience feelings associated with accomplishment in the wake of "lack of"s, resilience becomes like a drug they're taking for the malady of the challenge. There is a resiliency high that comes from excelling in the wake of the challenges one is faced with. This may very well explain how some of my foundational life experiences have caused me to become addicted to the resilience high and all of the feelings of accomplishment and satisfaction I felt early on in life. I am a resilience junkie, and I hope you will join me by opening yourself to experiencing this as you navigate the new world.

My experience with resilience fueled the essential, practical groundwork upon which I founded the notion of Techno-Resiliency. I have lived, felt, and seen the results of being both resilient and Techno-Resilient. Feelings of self-satisfaction and personal accomplishment are amplified when you do something and realize it wasn't because you were told you had to, but because you knew it was what needed to be done. You chose to rise to the occasion, no matter how challenging or impossible that occasion seemed. Those of you who are constantly beating the odds and accepting and conquering what seem like off-the-wall challenges in life are fueling that healthy resilience high.

But what if your resilience muscle is weak and underdeveloped? To strengthen resilience, you must be willing to dig deep, to soul search, and you must see failure as a learning opportunity. In my volunteer work coaching hockey players, I encourage them to regularly reflect on their performances in a journal. I also encourage them to embrace feedback with grace. You must not take for granted the idea that your organizational team members know how to accept and respond to feedback. Providing them each with a feedback journal and something that encourages them and allows them to offer thoughtful responses to feedback, as well as daily workplace reflections, is the type of higher-order thinking and business practice your organization will benefit from. Getting them to reflect on and share how they were able to overcome a particular challenge and how they felt when they did it is the type of intellectualized process that builds resilience in the intentional manner and capacity that you require. You must be willing to challenge all things you've previously taken for granted.

Resiliency Muscle Matters

An awareness that resilience has no meaning except in relationship to the desirable outcomes you want to achieve in your organization is fundamental. For this to happen, you need a "growth mindset" and not a "fixed mindset," advises Stanford psychologist Carol S. Dweck in the book, *Mindset: The New Psychology of Success.* If you have a fixed mindset, you are undermining your capacity for growth, creativity, intelligence, and success. You see these as static. You are inhibited by a fear of failure, and you avoid it at all costs as way of maintaining a sense of being smart or skilled at what you are doing and to maintain a sense of equilibrium. Now more than ever you need a growth mindset, which Dweck discovered thrives on the challenges of the day and does not fear failure—the kind of debilitating fear that comes from remaining static and being left behind in a new world that requires a high level of inspiration and innovation to get the job done.

Sports and working out have always been an integral part of my life. When I was young, my workouts were fueled by the typical young Canadian's dream to play in the NHL. Later in life, it was bodybuilding, and today, it is just for the health of it. To build muscle and strength, you need resistance. To build resilience, you also need resistance, and in a post-pandemic era, the world has become our global gym, where we can't resist resistance! It is there at every turn. Your challenge is to learn to use the resistance around you to build up your resilience muscle in this new world in which you operate. Today, you must take an athletic approach to enacting resilience within your organization. Resilience must be seen as an athletic endeavor, where the combination of swift action, strength of character, and a responsive and flexible guiding mental framework will determine your ultimate performance in the game of business. It must be developed and fostered at all times. In the wake of your new-world challenges, you need new-world thinking, and Yale University scholars Edmund Gordon and Lauren Song offer something compelling to think about.[4] In their many writings, they note that negative, constraining factors do not automatically result in depressed development. Their insights and research seem to support the old adage that what hurts you today makes you stronger tomorrow. In essence, hardships are not consistently associated with negative outcomes. Operating as catalytic agents of resistance, hardships can aid in building the resilience muscle Wharton psychologist Adam M. Grant advises must be built.

Developing muscle takes time, persistence, consistency, determination, teamwork, and a concrete, collaborative plan. Within the domain of the organizational culture, and in life itself, a Mandate to Great, powered by an omnipresent driving desire to be better, do better, and make others around you better, will make the world a better place to live and every organization a better place to work and thrive. The mandate must always be supported by an environment that is psychologically responsive and resilience building, through the awareness of how to both navigate and maximize the pervasive post-pandemic resistance you confront on a daily basis. However, it must be said that awareness is only the starting point. Understanding the new-world impact is critical; responding to it with a perspective of psychological resilience is vital. Just as Google executives see it as a must-have for developing their mandate for greatness in their team members, you must have a plan in place for how to build and sustain a psychologically responsive work culture that goes beyond meeting the emotional needs of your team. It must exceed them.

More than ever, you and your team have had to be resilient in

---

[4] Gordon & Song, 1994, p. 38

this post-pandemic time. Naturally, some team members will be more resilient than others. In the opinion Facebook leader Sheryl Sandberg shares in *Option B,* it's the strength and speed of your response to adversity that determines how resilient you are. Resilience can be built. It is a skill set. Grant and Sandberg advise that being cognizant of how you respond to adverse situations, how you feel, and what you have to do to overcome them is a starting point for building your inner strength and increasing your reaction time to adversity. Like an athlete, you must see resilience as something you have to train for. Once you *feel* resilience and you see the positive outcome from it, it becomes something intrinsic. It becomes the driving force behind the Mandate to Be Great you want members of your team to foster. Just like it guided, fueled, and elevated my actions early in my career when I had no direction or training, it can power your organizational greatness in any environment.

Pockets of Resilience: A Move to Get Collective

While much research on the topic of resilience has been focused on the capacity of individuals and their response to adversity, another take on it can be found in a compelling piece of research titled, "Advancing community resilience research and practice: Moving from 'me' to 'we' to '3D'." Embracing what is regarded as an "adaptive systems framework" for understanding resilience, lead researcher Melissa L. Finucane from the RAND nonprofit research organization and her many colleagues advise that the adaptive approach to resilience is focused on how crises can highlight avenues for improvement within a community, or for our purposes, any organization. As the title suggests, and as my research and the Mandate to Be Great will confirm, there is a need to shift from a "me" to a "we" perspective in order to fully unlock the collective power that can be had when we multiply the positive energy and spirit that exudes from those regarded as resilient.

Pockets of resilience are those people or departments within your organization that have heightened levels of productivity, organizational awareness, integrity, and efficacy. Those who are working in the pocket also have a markedly positive and inspirational approach to what they do. I noted in my research that these types of people and departments are often willing to share what they know, and know what they share. It's noteworthy that these same individuals are equally invested in lifelong learning. As your organizational superheroes, their moto is, "Do better. Be better. Make others better." Don't fear—when it comes to expanding the pockets of resilience in your organization, the Mandate to Be Great is your detailed macro-level blueprint for how to achieve this.

At the micro level, expanding these important resilience pockets begins by first recognizing where they are, or in some cases, at the individual level, whom they are, within your organization. Ironically, achieving the collective form for your organization also means you have to start by recognizing the singular: the self-motivated and self-determined person. Once you identify individuals in your organization who have a mandate for greatness, you then find ways to expand those pockets of resilience. Recognize and allow these leaders to interact, share, support, mentor, and elevate as many people as possible. As you do so, break down departmental barriers, replacing them with a no-boundaries approach to organizational success. You can enable these departments and individuals to cross-pollinate within your organization by breaking down departmental walls and allowing the insight and inspiration these individuals can offer others to be more easily spread across your team. You must enable these individuals to feel competent and *be* competent in their endeavors. This will serve to further entrench their desire to be exemplars and resilience mentors to others. I will forever remember one line from a song I always had to sing as a kid in my grandfather's church: "Hide it under a bushel? No! I'm gonna let it shine." When you find people within your organization who are exemplary in what they do, it is up to you to find creative ways to let them shine! Too often, these people and pockets of organizational resilience remain hidden and are never fully exposed to others within the organization. As you already know, as an organizational leader, you have many roles, and one of them is talent scout.

Having one, two, or more individuals in your organization with the power and willingness to inspire and make others want to inquire is a starting point. The critical piece here is that you need more than just focus on *self*. Would you be happy knowing your child's school has only one inspirational teacher in it? You need a collective vision, determination, and motivation. You need to foster many resilience captains and cheerleaders within your organization, allowing those with a natural capacity for resilience building to help move others forward.

The workflow for your organizational Mandate to Be Great starts with your commitment to be better, do better, and make those around you better. It flows through your desire to inspire a high level of "careness and awareness" at this most human of times through your responsive and upgraded post-pandemic human resources policies that foster resilience. The result of your own personal "careness and awareness" will be felt within your organization and lead to a sense of overall corporate wellness. From this point on, the mandate for greatness that you inspired is something that will become contagious, and what happens when coupled with an upgraded Techno-Resiliency skill set in the form of the "5 Traits" that will be detailed in the forthcoming chapter. These are the traits you'll offer your team as a template for working at home. When they're used in the office, team members will suddenly have the capacity to do more with less. With each step in forging these traits, you are building and strengthening a capacity for resilience, with the attention and intention it requires.

When your organizational metabolism has been stoked; your home work, mastered; your human resources team, working diligently to add the required level of "careness and awareness" to your policies; and there's a plan in place to expand the pocket's of resilience that exist in your agency, you are ready to move on to fostering the specific 5 Traits required to become fully Techno-Resilient.

Let's Get Techno... Resilient!

Have you considered the question, Can my organization learn? If you haven't, you need to, because what you discovered during the 2020 pandemic, and perhaps while reading the pages of this book, is that you and your organizational team have a lot to learn!

As a doctoral student in England, I intuitively connected my understanding of organizational learning to a schema that is best represented by the concept of *metabolism*. The notion of your organization having a metabolism can be a useful and intuitive metaphor. It will help you frame the context for learning in your organization. Viewing your organization in this way recognizes that it may be slow to change, much like my metabolism has been of late. As I get older, I try to accelerate my metabolism with a revamped diet and an accompanying plan to eat better and work out more…though the change comes slower than it once did. Much like a metabolism, your organization is likely sensitive and slow to change. Finding the right balance and maintaining that metabolic state, if you will, takes ongoing work. There is no doubt your organizational metabolism has slowed down in the wake of the pandemic. Now you simply need to know how to effectively stoke it.

The metaphor of an organization having a metabolism is my unique conception, but the idea itself has a theoretical structure that's built upon the 1993 research and writings of scholars like Noam Cook and Dvora Yanow, who advise that the use of the term *organizational learning* prompts the question, Can organizations actually learn? The answer is most certainly yes. The key distinction in their work is the need for you to hold a cultural view of organizational learning, as opposed to the more traditional, cognitive-based understanding. A cultural view asserts that your organization must set, maintain, and continually refine your values and intellectual standards, which can be shared by the collective. While these scholars do not refute the contribution made by the cognitive perspective, they do suggest that a cultural perspective helps avoid some of the difficulties they report being associated with the cognitive approach. In their research, they identify challenges that are a result of understanding the organization from the perspective of individual cognition:

- Due to the fact the cognitive perspective utilizes an understanding of learning from theories about individuals, one must be able to demonstrate that organizations actually learn like an individual. It has not been established that organizations do learn like individuals!
- The study of individual learning is a complex endeavor, largely bound by many theoretical constraints. To explain these in relation to how an organization learns adds a new level of complexity to the research that has not been adequately accounted for.

Simply put, it is not clear how two such dissimilar things as individuals and organizations could carry out identical activities.

Ironically, the notion of metabolism is based upon an individual state of functioning. However, this is where the comparison and thinking around the organization and its structure as being singular in nature ends for some scholars, and for you. Instead, similar to Noam Cook and Dvora Yanow, who in their research paper titled "Culture and Organizational Learning" stated, "Learning is understood to be done by the organization as a whole, not by individuals in it…"[5] The concept of understanding how your organization learns through the metabolism metaphor is better thought of as *the metabolism of the organization*. Your organization learns as a collective, and stoking your organizational metabolism assumes having only two people in your organization with their metabolisms stoked is not good enough. You need an organization where everyone in it has their metabolism stoked and is therefore able to run at maximum calorie-burning efficiency.

The ultimate responsibility for enabling and cultivating a resilient working environment rests with you. Those who rely on you are counting on you to lead by example, judging you daily not by your policies, but by the responses and action, not *inaction,* that naturally flow from them. Any plan for building true Techno-Resilience must come in the form of living and breathing documents that foster your organization's metabolism. Not the kind of policy that sits dusty and outdated in a shiny white policy binder, but one that is both created and embraced collectively. You must have your finger clearly on the pulse of your organization in this new post-pandemic world. This is how you will build and sustain a Mandate to Be Great within your organization.

---

[5] S.D. Noam Cook, Dvora Yanow. "Culture and Organizational Learning - S.D. Noam Cook, Dvora Yanow, 2011." SAGE Journals. Accessed February 10, 2021. https://journals.sagepub.com/doi/abs/10.1177/1056492611432809.

Overcome versus Overcoming

If you've ever been to Lancaster in the UK, you know it looks much like a Sherlock Holmes movie. The cobblestone streets and the black cast-iron lampposts that line the winding roads cast some dim light on the castle that is perched on a hill overlooking the town. Until very recently, I was told it served as the town jail. Only in hindsight do I appreciate my time studying at Lancaster University and the experience of learning at one of the world's top universities with people from around the globe. It has connected me to some very deep thinkers and other amazing people. However, while I was immersed in my studies, there was little time and energy to explore and appreciate the landscape and the people. To be honest, it was something I never imagined or planned on doing. It was also one of the most challenging things I have ever done! I recall several times on my academic UK journey almost being overcome by the experience, emotional highs and lows, and the monumental task of completing the PhD program while also working full time as a university professor who was both teaching and publishing. Added to this was the stress of trying to balance family life with two young children and support a wife who also had a demanding profession. In life and in business, it is a matter of overcoming or being overcome by the challenges you confront and the adversity you unwittingly face.

While "inspiration as innovation" will need to be the new social currency, it is going to be equally as important that workers and people in general possess a level of Techno-Resiliency that will enable them to navigate workplaces that may be confronted with any "lack of"s (resources, finances, training, motivation, technology, information, customers, collaboration). As revealed earlier, Techno-Resiliency means cultivating your capacity for thriving as a technology-enhanced workplace by maximizing existing resources and team efficiencies while minimizing costs and complexities. It is a teaching based on three decades of research and educational experience.

Today, the same question that drove me years ago, as a doctoral student, to the development of my concept of Techno-Resiliency has taken on an even greater importance for you. The question is this: How are some professionals able to overcome a lack of financial resources, support, training, and up-to-date technology, and still have a profound impact on the learning with technology? A focus on actual work practice and not on the unseen (what is going on in the head) is where I chose to focus my research—those actions and inactions that your leadership and success are judged and dependent on.

A second question has since emerged, and it is interconnected to my original research on Techno-Resiliency. It requires a "widening of the lens," and it merely takes the technology out of the equation. That question is this: How and why are some businesses going to overcome the considerable challenges and "lack of"s they are going to face going forward? The answers provided to the first question within this book will also inform the answer to the second question. There is an inherent and important correlation between the two. In the new world, you must continually seek answers to these questions for your organization's continued growth and vitality, and for you to be and continue to be Techno-Resilient. Print the questions off and post them on your wall for a constant reminder of your need to focus on resilience building.

Thriving as a workplace in this new world will require higher levels of self-determination by all and a skill set that is best defined and understood as being Techno-Resilient. In the upcoming 5 Traits of Techno-Resilient People and Organizations section of this book, I will reveal some specific strategies for overcoming the "lack of"s that you are sure to face as you use your new-world GPS that is still searching for some waypoints to help you navigate uncharted terrain.

When your entire team commits to the Mandate to Be Great, your organization's metabolism will be fueled by a steady diet of support, inspiration, and collaboration. It will all happen in a work environment that enables employees to feel and be competent at what they do. They will see how the diet works through you, as you will be the exemplar of it, and not just the presenter of it. You must lead by example. This steady and consistent diet that you and your team will enjoy together will build the Techno-Resilient muscle that when flexed will be able to lift the weight of this new world!

The Science Behind Techno-Resilience

Techno-Resiliency was born out of the belief that *resilience can be taught*. The theory and practice of Techno-Resilience has grown from the observation and study of work practices that allowed professionals in an educational organization to overcome considerable challenges when others in similar settings were not doing so.

While I chose to shine the spotlight on "resilient professional practices" when it comes to technology use, researcher Norman Garmezy was the one who most inspired me, as he originally proposed a "resilience/vulnerability" model. Garmezy's focus was on child development. His theory was simple in nature, yet not so simple from a research perspective. His work looked at children who were living in socially impoverished (vulnerable) conditions with a bid to follow them through life to see how and why some individuals were able to overcome certain "barriers" in order to become successful and contributing citizens (resiliency).

Garmezy's desire to learn from these individuals in a bid to share the "life-coping skills" he pinpointed through his research was noble; you can imagine the complexity of his research. His goal was to help others by offering, through local social-service agencies, training to vulnerable individuals on how to use the coping mechanisms he discovered in his resilient population. His research and the intention behind it resonated deeply with me, and more than twenty years after I was first exposed to it as a graduate student in the field of child development, it became the foundation upon which I successfully built my own theoretical house (albeit with a few important structural and cosmetic changes, to keep up with the Joneses!). I began to question what would happen if the notion of vulnerability were to be removed and we accept the idea that the concept of resiliency, when better understood, can help elevate us and better inform us during this period in history when people and organizations are looking for inspiration and support. Are there, in fact, lessons that can be learned from those who are resilient? Is it possible that a spotlight on "resilient professional practices" specific to technology use can serve as some of the inspiration that becomes the "innovation"? My research has shown that it can.

Techno-Resiliency in its original conception is the ability to find creative solutions with limited resources and supports to make learning better with the integration of technology. Today, the broadened definition reflects the need for Techno-Resiliency in all agencies, businesses, and our day-to-day living, recognizing it as a generalizable concept. However, it is important to appreciate that in regard to the concept itself, Techno-Resiliency is more of a journey than it is a destination. In its more global definition, Techno-Resiliency is the ability to find creative solutions to technology-related problems with limited resources and supports to positively impact one's working environment and life. It encompasses the technological realm, but perhaps even more importantly, the psychological and emotional realms.

With the move to online learning and work-related platforms that has rapidly taken place over the past years, those who are Techno-Resilient have been able to overcome some of the "lack of"s in terms of the lack of support, training, and understanding about how to teach and work in this new domain—however, not all of them. There are many who have struggled immensely with the pressure to replicate and deliver a classroom learning experience or a synchronous business meeting with multiple participants on a glitchy, unfamiliar platform. The view changes considerably when your office window becomes the screen of your laptop. As the famous sociologist Peter Berger noted, we must always be challenging our "worlds taken for granted" in a bid to advance our thinking and insight. I don't think Berger realized when he wrote that in the 1960s that someday every aspect of our largely taken-for-granted world and lives would be challenged. Now the question is, Are you up for the challenge?

You've already taken the first step in awakening Techno-Resiliency in your organization. It is becoming aware of the fact that this revolutionary mental framework and accompanying skill set actually exist, and is grounded in having an organizational Mandate to Be Great and a desire to inspire and be inspired. The second step is providing training to your team to help them elevate and achieve true Techno-Resilience through the development of the 5 Traits of Techno-Resilient People and Organizations. These traits provide an action-oriented process for understanding how to problem-solve and work in a technology-enabled home or office space, often with limited guidance and resources. They provide you and your team with the ability to feel effective and to *be* effective! Once they are adopted, the final step is to ensure you are providing a psychologically responsive workspace that allows your team to feel supported and connected, and affords them a sense of autonomy. The ultimate objective is for you and them to be mentally free enough to get the job done in a world where the senses and mental acuity have been dulled by the chaos that surrounds us.

According to Irving Seidman in his book *Interviewing as Qualitative Research,* "The primary way a researcher can investigate an educational organization, institution, or process is the experience of the individual people, the 'others' who make up the organization or carry out the process."[6] In my ten years of working with over five thousand individuals, and through years of research, I found that there was a set of organizational intellectual standards, combined with some unique cost-effective and collaborative team-teaching practices that were intentionally enabled by the organizational leader, combined with an obvious professional imperative by employees (now termed the Mandate to Be Great) that worked in harmony to achieve outcomes that other organizations with so much more money and available technological resources simply could not achieve. Through years of research and practice, the following five character traits have been identified as universally applicable to creating Techno-Resilient leaders, whether they be educational authorities, teachers, students, parents, or—most predominantly—a corporate leader like you. They are those that spur a Mandate to Be Great into true Techno-Resilience in businesses, in organizations, and in day-to-day life.

---

[6] Seidman, page 9, 2013, paraphrased.

The 5 Traits of Techno-Resilient People and Organizations:

Trait 1: A Mandate to Be Great
*Have and build a driving professional imperative within your team!

Trait 2: No What, No How, but You Had Better Know Where!
*Address your "no how" with "know-how."

Trait 3: Barriers + Bridges = Breakthroughs
*Find a "meta-for" moving from *overcome* to *overcoming.*

Trait 4: Build a Drive to Thrive
*Be in command of your mentor "ship."

Trait 5: Create a Kingdom of FREEdom
*Develop a low-cost, user-friendly internal capacity.

Perhaps more than any time in your history and legacy, you are looking for results that can make a difference in your organization. Now, more than ever, Techno-Resilience can serve as that elusive X factor that we are all going to be looking for as leaders, as organizations, as communities, and as a global society. However, it will be very important for us all to realize we are not chasing a dream here; we are chasing an experience and actively participating in an evolution. In his book *Summary: The Infinite Game,* global leadership expert and founder of *Start With Why,* Simon Sinek wants us to see Techno-Resiliency as a journey, not a destination. Enabling Techno-Resilient practices in your organization and in your life will have an indispensable outcome: You will have become fully Techno-Efficient. And instead of *being* overcome, you *will* overcome.

If you're ready to begin becoming truly Techno-Resilient, let's dive into the 5 Traits!

THE 5 TRAITS OF TECHNO-RESILIENT PEOPLE AND ORGANIZATIONS

Trait 1

A MANDATE TO BE GREAT

magine your organization operating on all cylinders, with individuals and teams fueled by a high-octane mandate for greatness. For organizational leaders like you, this is an ultimate objective: to have employees devoted and unapologetically dedicated to the goals and ambitions of the company, willing to learn and to do their specific jobs at the highest level possible, and willing to overcome challenges they face, not be overcome by them. How much would you agree to invest to have this? There are organizations outside of the educational establishments I've researched that have an employee base just like this, and the investment made by the management team is not measured in monetary figures. These leaders simply made an investment in their *people* to achieve it. All Techno-Resiliency begins with a Mandate to Be Great, making this the first of the 5 Traits of Techno-Resilient People and Organizations. In this section, you will be given a foundational set of guidelines and research-based insights on what is needed from you and from your organization to start fueling a Mandate to Be Great in your team members that goes beyond mere self-motivation.

In my hometown, there is a local mining company called Cementation. It is the regular recipient of local and national awards for its outstanding business practices and support of its employees, and it is recognized as one of the top one hundred businesses to work for in Canada. It's not surprising that it continues to receive accolades and honors for its innovation in the mining industry. Forever curious about the inner workings of Cementation and its cult-like following by those who work there, I contacted Sarah (pseudonym), the wife of a powerlifting buddy of mine, who'd recently left her accounting position to work at Cementation. I was after some informal, qualitative-based insights about her experiences there. What I didn't expect was what she told me about "the heart of the matter."

Early in our conversation, I was struck by Sarah's emotion and devotion as she spoke about the management team and the staff she was working with. As we talked over a piping-hot cup of Earl Grey tea, it quickly became evident to me that it is the leadership team and the supporting cast of managers at Cementation that is acting as the *extrinsic* driver. These leaders are an essential part of fueling the Mandate to Be Great for the company's workers. Sarah spoke of an open, flexible, and nonconditional approach taken by managers who do more than just listen; they respond. What immediately came to mind for me was the fact this company has established an *emotionally* and *psychologically* responsive work environment. Cementation provides the necessary energizing stations for its workers in the form of an empathetic management team and a *worker-centric* human resources staff. They have policies in place that quite simply *meet needs*.

The most memorable part of our conversation for me was listening to Sarah recount the commitment and attention to detail taken by the management team in putting on the annual Cementation Christmas party. The party has become legendary within the local community because of how thoroughly it showcases a recognition (and almost spoiling!) of its employees. The Cementation party is the envy of many employees from other organizations. Featuring top-notch live musical entertainment, the event recognizes in a heartfelt manner the efforts of team members. Comradery takes precedence over any politics or personality clashes. Their parties are package, with people and with energy.

Building an internal Mandate to Be Great starts with your actions. It must then flow through responsive and supportive policy mechanisms that allow employees the mental reprieve they will need in the new world's workplace. Every team member needs to know help is available when required. Just like at Cementation, policies must quite simply meet needs. That said, this is not just a one-way street you are traveling. It can't be. You need to receive something back in the form of a deep-set professional imperative that will get the job done, whether it be from home or the office. You will receive this when you consistently strive to build a supportive and inspirational work culture. Individuals with a professional imperative are more than just intrinsically motivated to get the job done; they are also willing to inspire, to share, and to learn with others. This is a significant upgrade in attitude and skill set.

The beginning of the Employment section of Cementation's website reads, "What if a company's goals aligned with those of its employees? It sounds simple, but what it really means is a unique company that puts people before profit." When I read this, I slid back into my chair, looked up, and started to laugh. From the standpoint of a researcher, I felt they could not have made it any easier to understand what is really going on at Cementation: "people before profit." The very essence of what fuels a Mandate to Be Great within an organization had quite literally jumped off the screen and slapped me in the face! There was now no question for me in regard to the how and why of Cementation's success. They are practicing what I mentioned earlier in this book from leadership teachers like Simon Sinek and Jim Collins: their people come first.

The Mandate to Be Great is a professional imperative at the broader macro level. It includes supporting the unstated day-to-day operations (tacit) and the stated (non-tacit) business operations and policies. Much like Cementation has done, the employees and the leadership team have forged the mandate together. The driving professional imperative at the individual level is something similar to, but more intense and intentional than the old-fashioned work ethic that Grandma and Grandpa preached and demonstrated. For many of the professionals I have researched, the professional imperative was deep-set, driving, intentional, and arguably at the highest level of whatever rating scale you want to use. They were driven to be better and do better.

Be the Prophet and Profit!

Cultivating an organizational Mandate to Be Great and realizing you want those in your business to be driven by this professional imperative (and not a lower-level form of self-determination) starts with you. Having such a mandate results in a willingness by others for collaboration, a willingness to do more with less, a willingness to do it because it needs to be done, coupled with a capacity for solving problems, inspiring others, and inspiring innovation. The Cementation organizational team is fueling this highly desirable commodity by putting people before profit. What they are doing supports everything I have written to this point and puts a successful business face to it.

Back in 1998, Jeffrey Pfeffer of the Harvard Business School published a compelling book titled, "The Human Equation: Building

Profits by Putting People First." As a highly esteemed professor of organizational behavior at Stanford University, Pfeffer presents considerable and convincing evidence through scholarly research and a series of case studies that a company like yours can gain a sustainable and competitive edge by putting your people first. You do this by realizing your team is the most valuable resource and asset you have. You then treat them as the most valuable resource you have. Pfeffer advises that a workforce that feels and sees tangible evidence of a committed employer will be more productive and will be willing to act as a partner with the agency. The "human equation" about which he writes has only become more complicated and important to solve in this post-pandemic world.

As a business leader, you know the value of collaboration and its intimate connection to its close cousin: innovation. But do you also recognize the need for what I call "collaborative success" in your organization? The leaders at Cementation surely do. Collaborative success is guided by a collective, corporate Mandate to Be Great—one that shares the wealth with the organizational team when times are good and continues to care and support when times are challenging. It also provides a setting where good mental health for all members of the organization is valued. Going back to the metabolism metaphor, collaborative success realizes that when one part or multiple parts of the organizational body are not well, the entire metabolism of the organization can be disrupted. During my research into what it was like to work at Cementation, it was brought to light that employees receive a considerable bonus each year. When times are good, the wealth is shared; however, at all times, the organizational health is never jeopardized.

Going back to my early studies in child and development, I could say the workers at Cementation are "securely attached" to the organization. In simple psychology, attachment is an enduring emotional bond. In my mind, and in the context of an organization, it is pure and simple allegiance. However, the notion of "secure attachment," pioneered by renowned British child psychiatrist John Bowlby, more or less states that a child who is securely attached feels understood, feels secure, and is calm enough to allow for the optimal development of the central nervous system. The questions you can ask yourself are these: Do your workers feel understood and secure, and are they calm in the wake of adversity so the organization and the individual can operate at an optimal level? Is the metabolism of your organization where you need it to be? These are the elements of people and organizations characterized by the first trait of Techno-Resilient people and organizations: a Mandate to Be Great.

In the teacher interviews I conducted for my PhD research, I discovered candid insights as to what was driving the resilient use of technology-enhanced teaching and learning (TETL) in the educational organizations studied. The professionals in these schools seemed to exhibit, in both practice and conversation, a steadfast and focused commitment to the goal and the duties of achieving a level of engaged technology integration for their students, in spite of existing technological and financial barriers. The question you have to ask yourself is, Where did this commitment come from, and how do I replicate it, fuel it, and refuel it within my organization?

In both the observed practices and the conversations I had, all of those studied seemed to exhibit an unwavering determination. They were unwavering in their goal to provide an engaged level of technology use for their students in spite of existing technological and financial "lack of"s. In my research, there was another "working gear" that members of the organizational team had that I uncovered. It drove the work practices and the notion of Techno-Resiliency. Having the awareness and capacity to develop a Mandate to Be Great within an organization was (and is) crucial; however, my research revealed that the catalyst for this commitment came from a combination of organizational drivers.

Two intrinsic drivers emerged through an interrogation of the interview data: a professional-based driver and a student (employee)-centered driver. Throughout the investigation, it never appeared that technology was driving the practice of the educators; rather, the practice was being driven by a prominent professional imperative: a desire to do better, to be better, and to make those around you better. More precisely, having a Mandate to Be Great appeared to exist at two separate, yet arguably connected levels. The first level was centered upon the desire of the educators to remain current and relevant in their professional practice, while the second level was student-centered. The educators expressed a resolute commitment to assuring students that what they were teaching had relevant and functional twenty-first-century skills related to TETL that would serve them in the future, while also ensuring students would not be at a disadvantage when entering higher grades.

In addition, there was another regularly cited and vital *extrinsic* driver: you, the organizational leader. The fact of the matter is, when I interviewed professionals, parents, and students, the principal was regularly cited as being the catalyst for enabling and fueling the greatness that everyone was feeling and seeing the results of. In this organization, the results were not based on profit margins—and not even on grades, for that matter. They were based simply on customer satisfaction. All this is to say that it starts with you. When you are the prophet, you profit! Through your regular day-to-day interactions, you model for your team the expected work ethic and standards for the level of interpersonal relationships you want your organization to have. You bring to life the philosophy "people before profit." Leaders like you are regularly judged on their actions, reactions, and interactions. However, you must realize you are also judged on your inaction.

As a drummer in a rock band, I am familiar with an old adage that states, "It is often what you don't play that says more about your drumming than what you do play." I have taken this to heart in my own playing in the classic-rock cover band MLC. I do my best to front our band with a steady, unwavering backbeat, devoid of unnecessary fills and anything that might distract from the flow of each song. I hit hard, I don't play over the guitar leads, and my drums are regularly tuned to sound good. I know I am doing my job as a drummer when the dance floor is full, and it generally is when our band plays! As a leader in your organization, you must act like a drummer, setting the beat for your organization with a steady and unwavering commitment to people first. Make sure you are in tune with your organization's emotional and psychological needs. When you do this, your organization's dance floor will be filled with enthusiastic and energetic team members dancing to the hypnotic beat you are driving. Oh yes, and just know that everybody loves a good drummer!

Key Steps for Success

The inspirational and supercharged work environments I noted in my research, as well as the one I highlighted at Cementation, have mostly achieved their success by putting their people first. But you need deeper insights and something more to work from. Putting people first is like the sun-filled skyline in the big, beautiful picture, one that necessitates a closer look.

Earlier in this book, I mentioned the research performed by Adam M. Grant and Jihae Shin on the nature of self-determination and motivation in the workplace. They noted three psychological needs that must be met in order to achieve self-determination and a level of worker motivation: 1. Autonomy. 2. Competence. 3. Relatedness. In our new world, we need more than the self. It's time to put the self on the shelf. What is important for you to realize is, the same conditions these scholars identify for enabling motivation and self-determination are the same ones that can be used for fuelling the professional imperative in your team. They simply need to be translated to the collective whole, touching upon the desire to inspire and to be inspired.

I have seen these principles at work, and I have felt them inside the organizations I've researched. I've also regularly heard about how these same conditions were influencing (for better or for worse) the practices in the organizations at which the more than five thousand university students I taught were working. In class, we would regularly reflect on their practicum experiences during my TETL course. We would try to determine how they could achieve a level of Techno-Resiliency that would allow them to inspire others in the workplace, as well as a desire to overcome the challenges they were sure to face. The goal was to make them a contagion designed to spread a Mandate to Be Great.

During those many important conversations and explorations, it was ultimately determined that in order to overcome many of the technology-related challenges and "lack of"s that were repeatedly being cited as areas of concern, an understanding of the simple phrase "Attitude equals altitude" was imperative. As I detailed in my lectures, elevating your attitude is accomplished by understanding a second, quirky little mantra: "If you hang with turkeys, you will never fly." The fact of the matter is, as I learned in my research and through many discussions with thousands of students in the Faculty of Education, overcoming starts with a keen desire to want to overcome, and it is fueled by hanging out with other like-minded individuals. This is one of the most elemental understandings I can offer anyone. While it is important to inspire others, it is equally important to find inspiration that can move you toward greatness in your life and in the workplace. Having a Mandate to Be Great is not simply something to be shared, but also something that should be felt throughout the organization.

You can achieve such a feeling by doing as I once did when teaching: model Techno-Resiliency in action. At the onset of every class, I would declare "Dr. G.'s Techno-Resilient Moment." In a bid to model and induce a spirit of creativity, imagination, and resourcefulness (all the aspects of being Techno-Resilient), I would present my students with an older piece of technology that I had picked up at a garage sale or thrift shop. I would then demonstrate how this technology could be used to enhance teaching and learning. Oftentimes, I'd spent no more than ten dollars on the item! Through the showcase, I was able to debunk the idea that technology integration has to be expensive—a concept often cited as a concern and barrier by many of my students.

Later in the year, "Dr. G.'s Techno-Resilient Moment" was turned over to the students. At this stage of the process, I would present them with a cost-effective and often outdated technology I'd once again found in a thrift shop. Working in groups, they would attempt to discover, uncover, and refine ways of making inspired use of it in their teaching practice. I'd modeled for them how to make something from nothing, and now it was their turn to see what they could do. Working in groups, they had the power of "we" and an important shared purpose and mandate to overcome. The results of these explorations and conversations were truly remarkable. In the end, I was able to plant the seeds of Techno-Resilience within thousands of students-turned-teachers. There is no monetary value that can be placed on having inspired people in your organization who desire to "soar with the eagles" rather than being content to "hang with turkeys." You must be willing to model for your employees the same inspired and committed approach that you want in return. This is a must-do.

In a world where time is money and you are likely making up for lost time, you are seeking that magical elixir that can be easily consumed in a bid to make it all right. This isn't that. This work is about creating the optimal conditions for enabling the Mandate to Be Great in your organization and fueling that professional imperative. It takes time, and it takes nurturing, though it will also equip you to navigate and thrive through all forthcoming seismic shifts!

When creating my program and body of corporate consulting work, I hesitated to offer the 5 Traits of Techno-Resilient People and Organizations as a linear "Steps for Success" framework, because they don't and won't work that way. Techno-Resilience requires starting with the big picture and a guiding principle of "people before profit." Don't just say it or write it down for everyone to see. As the drummer in your organization's band, you must play it loud for your audience to hear! Creating a Mandate to Be Great is only the first part of establishing that psychologically responsive and aware working culture that I have been referring to throughout this book. The following list offers important organizational 'must haves':

1. Your organization's team members need to feel they have some level of discretion in what they do and how they do it. With home work fast becoming the new norm, it is imperative that the boundaries and limits of this discretion are clear and well-established. Unlike in a home-based working environment, autonomy is sometimes stifled in an office-centric workplace. It is more naturally enabled for workers who are

at home. Don't take anything for granted in this regard. Recognize the need for autonomy as a preexisting factor for establishing the Mandate to Be Great, support it, and frame it. Do this through regular communication and by enabling the autonomy with the required technological and emotional supports. Recognize that when your team members are working from home, you need them to be autonomous, but this does not mean you want them to be disconnected from others. You must also recognize that they will need a specific skill set to work autonomously. The upcoming traits will provide these skills.

2. With many of your team members now working from home, you need them to also have a high level of Techno-Efficiency. Research shows they want and need to feel competent and effective in what they do. Their feeling this way will also help to fuel the Mandate to Be Great. However, you can't simply take for granted that everyone on your team has what it takes to be effective in this new working world. In fact, it is very likely many of your team members are not equipped with the mental and hard skill set required to be effective in the home work setting. Equip them with what they will need to feel and be effective! Giving them the tools to *feel* and to *be* is your job, and when you do it, you will bring them one step closer to unleashing an intrinsic mandate for greatness.

Enabling a Mandate to Be Great within others and throughout your organization requires that your team members feel connected to one another. At a time when your team may be working form home in isolation, and with more autonomy than ever, the reality is, a feeling of being disconnected can occur. Your role is to ensure it doesn't! In the upcoming chapters, I'll provide ideas on simple platforms that can support connection, though your guiding mandate will aid in this endeavor more than any other factor.

Digging Deeper

Let's go back to the question posed earlier: Where does a commitment to oneself, one's duty, and one's organization come from? We now have part of the answer from the narrative and the stories in this chapter. You need to provide some of the *extrinsic* motivation in the form of a responsive and supportive human resources policy and managers who do more than just listen; they respond. It is a combination and interaction of two key organizational drivers: one being *intrinsic,* and the other being *extrinsic.* In the people I researched, there was a very notable and driving *intrinsic* professional imperative that seemed to be contagious. As one educator told me, "I am willing to push myself to do this and learn this because I believe they will need to know how to use this technology when they go to college." For them, the organizational Mandate to Be Great was very much an altruistic endeavor. In terms of the second, extrinsic driver, you are the extrinsic contagion for greatness within the organization!

Having a Mandate to Be Great that is driven by altruism is like having the gold standard. Achieving this level of commitment and attitude from your team will not happen overnight. In some cases, your organization may actually need an enema. There is really no plainer way to put it. However, you need to know that if you achieve the gold standard in worker commitment in the form of a deep-set professional imperative, it will lead to higher levels of collaboration. In the organizations I researched, I had never witnessed higher levels of collaboration between educators, the leadership team, students, and even parents. The collaboration resulted in the sharing of resources, strategies, and important insights for how to make IT work in the wake of many "lack of"s. However, more significant than any sharing of information and insight is the sharing of a belief in one another, confidence, and inspiration. These elements are equally important if not *more* important than anything else you can share and inspire within an organization.

One of my taglines, highlighted earlier in this book, is "Inspiration is the new innovation." I believe it, and I have seen it in action. Remarkably, this altruistic and reciprocal-in-nature Mandate to Be Great I witnessed in others led to higher levels of *relationality* between workers, and the natural consequence was the sharing of information, skills, and inspiration. People entering the workforce all have a driving mandate and an ability to be Techno-Resilient in the same manner I've observed in others. You can't tell me that all of the people in the environments I've researched just *happened* to *have it*. I don't believe that. For some, it needs to be activated. You can act like the yeast in the bread-making process by establishing and modeling the organization's supported mandate. There needs to be a recipe for activating the intrinsic mandate within employees. For an organization like Cementation, one of the essential ingredients in their recipe is the provision of an emotionally and psychologically safe working environment that is enabled by a first-class human resources team that creates and supports *worker-centric* policies. I suppose it could be said that this is their yeast.

Today, more than ever, having a Mandate to Be Great will never be more noticeable or appreciated in a person and a workplace. For those who have it and bring it to the workplace, you will want to recognize it, nurture it, grow it, and quickly find ways for others to be around it. This inspiration is the new innovation.

A Mandate Minute

Techno-Resilient people are driven by an intrinsic desire to do better, to be better, and to make those around them better. Realizing that inspiration comes from being with and learning from others who are driven and action-focused. Techno-Resilient people look to be surrounded by other like-minded people. This essential characteristic is what fuels their willingness to overcome challenges, to go beyond the norm to troubleshoot ways of overcoming technological barriers, to share, and to ultimately care deeply about others and their daily duties. An organization that is regarded as Techno-Resilient recognizes the need to inspire and to fuel this deep-set professional imperative in others that is the foundation of a Mandate to Be Great. At the corporate level, it is a contagion for organizational success and innovation.

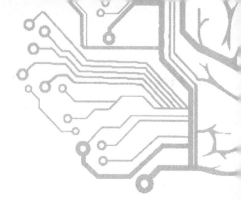

NO WHAT, NO HOW, BUT YOU HAD BETTER KNOW WHERE!

In today's world, time is a factor of nothing. And what you learned in the last chapter is that what will never change at any time in the operation of your business is the need to put your people before profit. Your business has hopefully continued to evolve its practices in order to keep ahead of the times, because just keeping up with the times is never good enough. In Trait 2 of the 5 Traits of Techno-Resilient People and Organizations, you will be exposed to a new way of thinking about the nature of information and knowledge that continues to elude many, despite the fact that it is an integral and pervasive part of our daily living and work culture.

The second trait is No What, No How, but You Had Better Know Where! If this does not make sense the first time you read it, keep reading it until it does: *No What* and *No How* have been replaced by *Know Where!* In a virtually connected business world, where time is money and locating the proper information takes time, your team needs some intellectual standards for how to navigate the online information vortex. You may not always know what you need or how to get there, but you must always know where you are going. This principle is based on the simple reality that today, many are wasting valuable time, energy, and money focusing on remembering the *what* and the *how* to do things, when it could be much more beneficial to develop the *know where* to find the information you need to know, when you need to know it.

I am not suggesting there is no need for the capacity to remember and recite information. Ask any math teacher, and they will tell you a student's success is still largely predicted by their ability to memorize the multiplication table! However, when you are looking at moving from a level of Techno-Resiliency (a willingness to overcome and not be overcome by "lack of"s) to a level of Techno-Efficiency within your organization, keep in mind that one of the skills I found in those I researched was their ability to skillfully locate and authenticate information they needed in a bid to support, in a timely manner, their *need to know* and get the job done. Your home workers need clarity, understanding, and a clearer pathway to the information they will need to get the job done with a high level of Techno-Efficiency, the ultimate objective and result of a truly Techno-Resilient person or organization.

You don't need to fill your brain with useless information in a virtually connected world. There is way too much other stuff going on in our lives today that is consuming valuable time, energy, and mental space. When my daughter comes home from school and informs me she has to memorize lots of information for a test, I am always curious to see what exactly it is she has to memorize. Most of the time, it is mundane information that really has limited long-term value for helping her in her studies. Sure, the process of having to learn how to study and commit information to memory is a valuable exercise; however, this process alone, when repeated hundreds of times by students, often leaves them to wonder, *What is the purpose of this?* When your child has to ask, "Why do I need to memorize this?", chances are, the teacher does not even have an answer! However, an exercise that requires students to learn how to validate and authenticate which facts are real and which are fiction, and how to determine this needs to be done, takes the fact-finding mission and learning to a whole new level: a twenty-first-century NEThical level of thinking. I have always loved the term *NEThics*—one that embeds the word *ethics* in the word *net*. There certainly is a need for a heightened awareness of what this means. In the development of this second trait, you are not only learning the facts; you are also learning how and where to find them, with the value-added aspect of learning how to validate and authenticate and them. What your team needs to know is, where to locate and how to authenticate information in the vast and serendipitously connected online quagmire of information. Knowing how to decode what is real and what is fake in the virtual realm has also become a critical skill.

In your new business, good old-fashioned *know-how* is supported and empowered by a revolutionized concept of *know where*. When your organizational *know-how* is supported by an ability to more efficiently utilize the vast wealth of online knowledge, in addition to a willingness and an ability to find other supportive and inventive ways of knowing, doing, and collaborating, you are now with the times. Then, to get ahead of the times, you need to develop even deeper understandings.

Bitten by a Shark

When I began writing this book, I decided the corporate examples I would include would come from the companies whose products I regularly see and use in my daily life. The story of how I was bitten by a shark is not as graphic or as traumatic as one might imagine. In fact, my having been bitten by this shark made my family life healthier and more efficient on many levels. Formerly known as Euro-Pro, the SharkNinja company has built an empire on their innovative and competitively priced vacuum and home appliance products. Our family owns and loves the Ninja air fryer that sits proudly beside my Keurig coffee machine! The Ninja air fryer takes far less time to cook foods, saves electricity, and most importantly for us, allows us to eliminate fried foods from our diet. This makes for a full, healthy family. However, in my opinion, the real superstar in their product lineup is the Ninja blender. It has been an essential part of my breakfast routine for many years. Each morning, my family can hear it spinning my magical elixir in the form of a spinach protein shake!

There is an important parallel that can be made between this company's rise to organizational fame and the innovative and inspirational concepts and strategies of No What, No How, but You Had Better Know Where! In an 2014 *Forbes* article, "How Shark Ate Dyson's Lunch in America," Leadership Strategy contributor Andrew Cave explained how the company's commitment to having a common way of working and thinking had been a game-changer. The leadership team knew how to best leverage insight, information, connections, and the metrics required to establish a vision and a plan to push them beyond the adversity they faced.

Similarly, you need the skills and the understanding that Trait 2 offers. Your knowing how and where to leverage the information and connections you need in the new world will help to galvanize your team and provide the metrics, clarity, and direction that the SharkNinja corporate leaders realized was missing. When you fuel this with a plan for establishing and cultivating a Mandate to Be Great and the skill set associated with Techno-Resiliency, you will have something truly revolutionary to guide your organization. From what I have come to see from the SharkNinja leadership team, they have acted like virtual sponges, soaking up all outside resources and maximizing available information in a bid to connect, collaborate, and innovate. In the new world, the ability to leverage available information and collaborations is an essential and powerful tool. The question is, Is information collaboration currently a tool in *your* business toolbox?

Beyond an Encyclopedia Mentality

I remember it well, sitting in the living room as a kid in the early 1970s as the encyclopedia salesman delivered his pitch to my parents. His expansive set of encyclopedias were strategically sprawled before him, the weight of the books pushing deep into our gold-colored shag carpet. I recall picking up one of the encyclopedias and feeling the heft of it in my hands, moving it slowly up and down to demonstrate to my parents its weightiness, and then slowly flipping through the thick, glossy pages. Sitting cross-legged on the carpet, I was mesmerized as I stumbled upon some colorful images of knights and castles that I fixated on for the duration of the sales pitch. To my great surprise, my parents actually bought the entire set! And it wasn't cheap.

Many people and organizations today are still using what I call an "encyclopedia mentality" years into the twenty-first century. Living in the past, they are employing an outdated framework for understanding and utilizing the valuable commodity of information. If you are not leveraging the abundance of available information from all media, and allowing for the co-creation and sharing of it within your business, you are losing ground.

What if I told you that you don't have to know it all? Would feel a sense of tremendous relief? Just imagine yourself having this conversation with a new employee on her first day: "Welcome, Taylor! To begin with…we don't want you to try and know it all. You can't possibly accomplish that, and you'd be wasting your time and ours if you even tried. Instead, we have set up what we call 'direct-connect' Share Hubs. These team-knowledge-sharing stations are linked to our intranet. And there, all of the answers to your questions are just one click away, regardless of whether you're working here in the office or from home. You will be able to connect with just about anyone in the organization via these portals. We also encourage you to share anything inspirational that is happening related to your work and build personal bonds. We especially want you to offer encouragement and insights to help others. This will be particularly useful if you are working from home, and you *will* be working from home until further notice. We've also made sure the answers to the questions are in a number of different formats, so that we're able to cater to everyone's personal learning style."

Ok, back to business earth now. What this story has to say is that you need to transform your online organizational community into one that is more than just a virtual connection to an online community where the information pathway is a one-way street! You need to attain the same level of sharing and caring that occurs in an office-centric workspace. You know this is possible, but is it happening, or at least on the way to becoming a full-blown reality? The answer is yes. However, it's not to the degree and at the level you need it to be, or to the degree that I believe it can and should be.

Within many of the educational organizations I have worked, researched, and studied in, the utilization, sharing, and distribution of information is still scattershot. The ability to efficiently locate and authenticate online information is what I call a *foundational twenty-first-century NEThical benchmark.* Creating virtual knowledge and personal-sharing communities where team members know they can go to get answers, timely support, and inspiration are critical for building Techno-Resiliency. These are skills that can and should be taught. Your online platforms need to effortlessly enable this to happen.

When my twelve-year-old comes home from school and tells me she is doing a research project and she does not know where to find information, I almost feel a sense of anger. When I ask her what the teacher advises she do, she informs me she is told, "Just Google it." As we covered in the chapter, "A Time with No Template," not every answer can come from a Google search, nor are many of today's complex organizational and individual challenges resolvable by casting such a vast net. The fact is, the "Just Google it" mentality poses some very serious problems for those not guided by some virtual-research skills or an inkling of *know where* (knowing where they need to look for answers). In a world of free speech, where everyone can write a blog and be an author, there are undeniable issues of reliability, credibility, and availability of information. It would be more suitable for a teacher to provide a framework and some deeper understanding and NEThical standards on how to navigate the internet, so students know where to search.

If I were instructing a group on how to conduct research on a specific topic, it would probably go like this: "Start by using a search engine that does some of the prefiltering for you. Use Google's Socratic to refine the content of your search. From there, you are going to use the following template I am providing you with to record your research questions and the information you find. You will note that within Socratic, there will be other information and websites that you can connect to regarding your initial search. When you find three websites that pretty much confirm and reaffirm one another's information, you will have formed a triangle, and we all know a triangle is a sturdy geometric shape!"

Years ago, I developed a process I call *online research triangulation* (ORT) to teach aspiring educators how to instruct students on proper online research skills. These realizations and skills should be an essential cornerstone of our teacher training and the skill set we are offering our students. They are equally as critical to your organizational team! Why are we still crowding our minds with useless information when time could be better spent teaching workers how to more efficiently locate, authenticate, and troubleshoot to find the information they need to know? Inside your organization, you must go well beyond "Just Google it"! You need a twenty-first-century skill set and framework for your team, now more than ever. By uniquely adapting the ORT principle and skill set to your company, your leaders can also be trained on how to more effectively locate and distribute the information that is needed to get the job done. Regularly updating your online platform to keep the pathways smooth and easily passable for the required and authenticated information is part of the solution. However, building the information pathways with two lanes so the information and inspiration can flow back and forth, and training your team on the value and the values that pave the way for this, is essential.

Your organization needs to establish virtual pathways to the information your team needs, adding another layer of Techno-Resiliency to your business operations. However, these virtual pathways must *not be* narrowly built, one-way, and essentially one-dimensional. You now know a powerful aspect of the collective Mandate to Be Great is the ability to inspire and to be inspired, to share and to care. Your virtual pathways must enable and cultivate the sharing of information and inspiration. Merely leading your team down a one-way virtual path to portals of information is misleading them.

Addressing and investing in a lack of employee *know-how* and replacing it with a *know where* approach of clear systems for answers and support, alongside a deep-set professional imperative that guides all employee actions, is sure to pay dividends when it comes to building a Techno-Resilient skill set!

A Mandate Minute

Techno-Resilient people have an awareness of, and are guided by a process for, how and why to navigate the internet and how to find information in a NEThical manner with a high degree of Techno-Efficiency. A highly Techno-Resilient organization takes nothing for granted and provides a twenty-first-century skill set and framework for how to navigate and leverage online resources using available information in a bid to heighten Techno-Efficiency, collaborations, innovation, and overall organizational proficiency. This same organization has in place strategies and processes for researching, exploring, and evaluating technologies before they are purchased, which we will explore further in Trait 5, Create a Kingdom of FREEdom.

Trait 3
BARRIERS + BRIDGES = BREAKTHROUGHS

When you think of a *barrier,* what do you think of? Do you think of something set in place that you can't and won't be able to overcome? People who are Techno-Resilient see and deal with barriers differently. Organizations that are Techno-Resilient also need to perceive and handle barriers in a different way. In Trait 3, Barriers + Bridges = Breakthroughs, you will be shown that sometimes it has to go beyond "mind over matter." Sometimes the matter has to actually be reconceived in order for you to get your mind around it!

Research shows that the commonly cited notion of "technological barriers" still predominates. If you don't believe me, simply go to the academic search engine Google Scholar and type in the words *technology* and *barriers.* What you will see is a laundry list of research that has been guided by the notion of "barrier" as part of the theoretical framework for understanding. In a research paper I copublished in 2012 in the *American Journal of Contemporary Research,* I noted that commonly cited barriers include many "lack of"s. The most common are a lack of funding, training, initiative, and support.

You will notice my intentional use of the words *inequities* or *"lack of"s* in place of *barriers*. This is a very purposeful and significant conceptual shift in language and in thinking. The commonly used language and focus on "technological barriers" found in research literature and in the workplace culture are debilitating for you and your organization. The problem with thinking of barriers as such is that it mentally sets you up for failure. It assumes an organizational inability to overcome and little or no desire by you and your team to scale the obstacles you face. There is a negative judgment about the work ethic and the abilities of everyone involved when the term *workplace barriers* is cast. When you really think about it, accepting the idea of something being a barrier assumes a person does not want to overcome it, or it is too big to be overcome

Back when I was defending my doctoral thesis, the term I used for barriers facing organizations was *organizational inequity*. I changed the term because I wanted to change the landscape and the thinking about what barriers were and how we perceive them. And to this day, I still do. When you really think about it, within and between organizations, there exist levels of inequity in funding, staffing, technology, and overall supports that propose the challenges... not "barriers" that are somehow moved into place and remain immovable from that place, preventing you from getting somewhere or at something. The real pioneering aspect of this change in thinking is the impact it is having on actual "doing" and overcoming in the workplace. Your conception of barriers is really all about moving from a place of feeling overcome by obstacles to overcoming them.

Today, the original notion of *organizational inequity* is more clearly conceptualized as *organizational "lack of"s*. This less blurry notion of "lack of"s better portrays the inequities (previously perceived as barriers) you have to face, deal with, and overcome every day. The following are some of the "lack of"s your organization may be confronted with, it may include a lack of:

- funding
- know-how
- technology
- vision
- resilience
- dedication
- innovation
- leadership
- collaboration

By thinking of and labeling these (or any other) inequities as "lack of"s, you avoid imposing a form of psychological judgment on your organization and your team members that viewing them as "barriers" may cause. A "lack of" can be resolved, whereas a barrier may seem insurmountable. Let me explain it to you the way I did to my thesis-defense panel. Viewing what is taking place within your organization today as a matter of "lack of"s places an onus on everyone to work together to cultivate and initiate the driving and deep-seated professional imperative (a Mandate to Be Great) that will lead you and your organization to find creative, innovative, and resourceful ways of overcoming and fulfilling the "lack of"s you are confronted with. Seeing and portraying these same challenges as barriers may cause you to assume you don't have the ability or the capacity to overcome the obstacle. This mental block can result in missed opportunities and efficiencies, should you and your team avoid or decide not to take on the task of surmounting the "barriers." The resilient spirit that I reviewed earlier in this book leads to overcoming, as opposed to being overcome. It is at the heart of the

Techno-Resilient work ethic and skill set you need to enable within your team.

In the new world in which you now live, work, and lead, your team will face many barriers, and you will need to overcome them, beginning with a shift in how you perceive them. In this new world, the real question is, Whom is the concept of a workplace barrier a meta-for? It is definitely not for you! Today, you are being called to have deeper insights and a seismic shift in your thinking about workplace challenges. You are also being called to shift your workplace practice, creating something more refined and adapted to a technology-enhanced organization that will guide you as you confront daily psychological and tangible barriers that for many *seem* insurmountable. You will be called to shift the metaphor of "workplace barriers" into a meta-for something bigger: an empowerment of your people to create the necessary bridges that lead the way from perceived barriers to powerful breakthroughs.

It's a Mental Game

The Techno-Resilient professionals I interviewed and worked with during my research and teaching career viewed barriers differently. They also saw their duty to others and the organization differently. Going back to some of my original research transcripts to demonstrate this, I found an excerpt from one very telling interview, which you'll find below. It speaks to the courage of the leadership team in allowing for the co-construction of a technology vision for a school organization, and it demonstrates how believing in your employee base can fuel and elevate your Mandate to Be Great to a level that allows people to take chances, to fail, and to overcome the "lack of"s, whatever they may be.

Our administration has always been supportive of us moving forward digitally, and really, really gave us the power to do that. That was another huge thing—that feeling of support and I'll talk—Dawn [vice principal] she always said to me, "I don't know how to use computers. I don't get it. I don't understand them, but I know that they're incredibly valuable and we need to be using them, so I'm going to support that as much as I can." And I think that's such a powerful attitude, as a teacher, to know: OK, she gets it, and I can go and do that. Tim [principal] before, the same way, Larry [principal] right now, same idea. You know, Larry came in and helped us set up a media lab, so we set up a lab where we've got fifteen iMacs. Yes, we could have bought a lot of PCs with that, but the iMacs are going to allow us to be the digital-media pioneers and move forward with it. The support that we've gotten in this building from our administration has really given us the reins, so to speak, to let us go and not always be successful, but to not have a fear of trying.

In this interview, urban school teacher, Jake (pseudonym) was enabled by the organizational leader to conquer a formidable barrier. It is a barrier we must all confront in these new and uncertain times: the fear of failure. This interview excerpt also identifies the high level of emotional support provided by the leadership team, as well as the level of responsiveness and commitment to making informed and prudent investments in technology when funds matter.

One of my many passions includes training young goaltenders as a goalie coach with Canada's fastest-growing hockey school, 360

Goaltending, a company owned and operated by former professional goaltender Dan Spence. In working with them, I've come to realize how important it is to teach our athletes about how mental the game of hockey really is! At training camps, I am tasked with running off-ice explorations and presentations for athletes and parents alike on what can be done to develop the crucial mental aspect of the position. The goaltenders in my camps aspire to play at a high level, and some even hope to reach the NHL. In order for them to be on track to reach their desired growth and skill targets, they must be taught to adapt and adopt a mental attitude that is able to overcome the many psychological barriers they must regularly confront head-on to play the position at a high level. Much like the goalies I work with, you must train yourself to see and feel "failure" and "obstacles" differently. This, coupled with an ability to overcome a common and debilitating psychological barrier in the form of a fear of failure, is something that must be addressed. Conquering them begins with a fundamental change in the daily language you use to program your mind, actions, and reactions to reach a point of there being mental barriers no more!

In 2014, I defended my doctoral thesis in front of a panel of European scholars at Lancaster University in the UK. In preparing myself for the occasion, I had to conquer many mental barriers in order to reach a point of being able to sit before them, confidently ready to defend my work. Even when I finally did feel ready, I remained faced with the common barrier we all face: a fear of failure. I conquered that lingering fear by focusing on the belief I had in my totally unique research concept (Techno-Resiliency), combined with a high level of preparedness. This intrinsic strength propelled me through the defense process.

What I found remarkable in my research and in my observations over many years is that building bridges to scale barriers within an organization, no matter what type of organization it is, starts with belief. This may seem ridiculously simple to state, and it is likely not a foreign concept to you, but it bears repeating that a belief in yourself and in those you lead is a contagion for organizational excellence. Belief fuels your ability to actually overcome "lack of"s (as opposed to *being* overcome *by them*), and the feelings associated with overcoming are powerful emotions that energize you and push you forward. While there are many who believe you must go forward fearlessly at all times, even in the face of adversity, I don't advise it! Fear is a natural emotion that acts to protect us in some cases. To go fearlessly may be a very difficult and unnatural thing for you to do. Based on what I have seen in my research and personally experienced it is better to go forward with a vision, an intention, a purpose, and a plan. By going fearlessly, you may be going blindly and unprotected. But it is important to always remember, as one of my wife's favorite advisers, Abraham Hicks, regularly shares, "Everything you want is just on the other side of fear." So, best to recognize the fear and persevere with a driving purpose and plan.

The Steps for Success

We have covered that changing our ability to overcome barriers begins with our belief in ourself and how we perceive the barriers themselves (as "lack of"s that can be overcome). The first step toward successfully shifting barriers into breakthroughs is establishing those bridges that link the two—those that take you from a point of feeling overcome to one of overcoming. It starts with the recognition there is always a capacity *within* you and others to be better, to do better, and to make those around you better. It's about coming back to what you instilled within yourself in Trait 1, by utilizing your Mandate to Be Great to fuel the transformation. True leaders sincerely believe in this mandate. When you set the bar high, it is amazing just how high people in your organization can and will jump, and how big the transformations can be when they do! I have seen it in my own life and work, and I have also chronicled it via my observations and interviews with those I've researched. Techno-Resilience was labeled as such because of a noted difference in how people subscribing to this belief respond to the "lack of"s they were dealt. Techno-Resilience is a bridge—though that bridge, like a muscle, must be built, which is what we are building toward with these steps.

Step two in the successful transformation of barriers into breakthroughs is conducting a *Techno-Resiliency "lack of" audit* to clearly identify the "lack of"s within your organization. However, there is a very important caveat that must be made when initiating and presenting this process to others within the organization. This exercise in chronicling organizational "lack of"s must be 100 percent guided by what is needed for your organization *as a whole,* to *be* better and *do* better! The concept of Techno-Resiliency is fueled by a desire to move beyond examining barriers, risks, and deficits toward a focus on developing positive and resilient aspects of your business practices. Moving from a focus on risk and barriers grounds business practice in hope and optimism, both of which are essential ingredients in building a high level of organizational motivation. Conducting a *"lack-of" audit* involves your talking, walking, and being an active listener with as many people as you can in your various departments and organization as a whole. Have your team leaders collaboratively develop a list of "lack of"s, starting with *must-haves* and ending with *wish-we-hads.* Ask leaders to consider all aspects of your business "lack of"s, including aspects of motivation, training, technology, office furnishings, and even staff parties! The audit must be an honest and open-ended process and appraisal. At the very heart of the matter, this is to be a concerted effort to find efficiencies and ways of supporting your team in a bid to get the job done and to get it done better, while becoming better individually and as a whole. Remember, Santa never promised you would get everything on your list, but there was something to be said for the excitement gained in the process of thinking about it, building it, and hoping that something on it just may arrive! Aim high, and audit with integrity.

Step three of the bridge-building process, as you journey from barriers to breakthroughs, takes you into familiar territory. This step is all about setting and prioritizing goals based on the consultation and information that is provided by the *"lack-of" audit*. Setting goals is a skill that can be learned. The fact of the matter is, very few have been trained to do it properly. For your *"lack of" audit*, it will be important to set a limited number of attainable goals. The goals you set should be measurable so that you will know if you've achieved them. There should also be a time frame for achieving them. In terms of the number of goals that should be set, there are differing theories on this; however, I advise keeping the total at two or three. Many people quickly lose sight of the goal of setting goals. In my mind, it is to feel and/or experience success when success in a particular area has been evading you. Part of the process must involve what I call the "steps for success" or the "who has to do what and by when" in order to achieve the desired outcome. In short, the goals set should be attainable and measurable, and individuals should know their role in helping to achieve them. Of course, every step continues to center around the shared Mandate to Be Great.

The next step, step four, is about you and your team becoming engineers as you begin to develop the blueprint and strategies for how to erect the mandate-based, micro- and macro-level bridges that need to be built within the organization to overcome the "lack of"s that are hindering your productivity. Much like with a tall, arching bridge, once the building has begun, it affords you an even greater perspective on where you are going and where you can go! In times when funding is tight and resources are scarce, you will need your team to consider all "outside the box" options in order to cut the "lack of"s list down. You will need to embrace and enact one of my favorite literary terms, *bricolage.* According to Merriam-Webster, this term, a noun, means "construction (as of a sculpture or a structure of ideas) achieved by using whatever comes to hand." The bridges you will build with your team in order to overcome the "lack of"s thankfully do not need to be built to any engineering standards or specific tolerances. They only need to be built to withstand the unique strains and loads your organization is facing.

Early on in my foundational work experience, I worked with an organization that was regarded in its time (more than twenty years ago) as one of the best intermediate-level schools in the area. I am regularly asked about what made this educational organization so great. My answer is always the same: the leadership team and the fact that every professional in the organization had high expectations for themselves and for others. Whenever somebody saw an equipment need, whether it be in the department of sports, art, physical education science, or technology, goals were set to acquire it and to *make IT happen.* And happen, it did. The students who were excelling were heralded as role models, given leadership roles, and asked to be exemplars for others. They were enabled to excel and were challenged to do so. Instead of the bar being lowered to a level that all could hurdle, it was set to an Olympic standard, if you will. When we did scale it, we accomplished something that mattered, something remarkable that everyone could be proud of. All students and staff members were encouraged to push their own personal boundaries, and personal bests were celebrated as if they'd qualified for the Olympics! If you prefer an analogy to mathematics in order for this to resonate, instead of bringing people down to the lowest common denominator, this organizational team opted to round up! The result was a work culture that was recognized for excellence in what we did, how we did it, and the outcomes that were achieved.

The questions that remain for you and your organization are, Are you rounding down or rounding up? Are you overcome, or are you overcoming your "lack of"s? Going forward, we need a seismic shift in thinking when it comes to the notion of technological "barriers" in the workplace, and, more generally, in our life space. To think of what must be overcome as "barriers" is to assume that most won't want to build a bridge to cross over them, nor do they have the capacity to do so. The goal is to overcome the obstacles we face in the workplace. I believe that in many work environments, and perhaps yours, most workers would like to hurdle the barriers with which they are confronted. They would like to embrace thinking of them as "lack of"s and pooling together to form innovative solutions that allow everyone to break through and thrive beyond them. With easy-to-navigate access to timely resources and the proper tools and skill set, you and your team will be able to cut right through the barriers or jump right over them. Start with the smaller, more surmountable "lack of"s if you must, and then build your belief and confidence in constructing the bridges that allow you to sail over the big ones.

A Mandate Minute

People who are Techno-Resilient see and deal with "barriers" in the workplace and in life differently. Guided by their resilient spirit and mindset, they are not afraid to try and overcome the barriers they face, and they are not overcome *by* them. This spirit is enabled and supported by a leadership team that views organizational barriers as mere "lack of"s. They recognize the internal and external capacity for collaborative and innovative solutions, as well as the opportunity to entrust and empower employees with getting the job done, sets the "belief bar" high. And, always, they are driven and fueled by a Mandate to Be Great.

Trait 4
BUILD A DRIVE
TO THRIVE

The 2020 pandemic provided us all with a great juxtaposition: intensified depersonalization and a social disconnect taking place as a result of social distancing, during a time when we have never been more virtually connected! Sociologists were left scratching their heads as to how we can progress as a collective society, and you were left wondering what it would mean for your organization as you scrambled to make sense of it all. You felt (and may still be feeling) the constraints of participating in office work, group activities, and gatherings while being unable to be face-to-face, the way you once were. Because of the mental and emotional strain that resulted from the pandemic, there has never been a time when your organization has required more connection with others. There has perhaps never been a time when you've needed to be as innovative as you do now, when it comes to determining how to move your organization together, collaboratively, in an effort to thrive once again. In Trait 4, Build a Drive to Thrive, your idea of what collaboration means for your organization will be reframed and displayed for you in a way that causes you to look at it much differently!

How does your organization connect or reconnect during a time of social disconnect? How do you collaborate and innovate when everything you are facing seems to frustrate? During times like 2020, there are countless questions that arise and new territory to be explored. These times can be exciting and provide opportunities for those leaders who are determined, passionate, and willing to not only think outside the proverbial box, but to also build something sturdier to weather forthcoming shifts and storms. What is that something sturdier you can construct to ensure your organization and its people can more securely and comfortably think and work within and outside of that box? The answer to this question begins with some fundamental insights on what collaboration really means for you and your team.

Techno-Resilient people and organizations know how to harness the power of collaboration and use it to build a collective Drive to Thrive. They are fearless in their quest to find ways to cut through the list of "lack of"s they are confronted with and seek to find innovative solutions that allow them to thrive, even in tumultuous times. One of the greatest tools of Techno-Resilience is the realization that you can never know it all. You, and everyone else, are constantly evolving and growing, and there is power in learning from and being connected to others who are committed to the task and can add valuable perspective. What matters is that your organization remains devoted to bringing your team together and how it does so, even when workers are physically far removed from your office headquarters.

Trait 4 of Techno-Resilient people and organizations is about knowing the value of collaboration when it comes to sustaining success through any waters, charted or uncharted. It is about not being fearful or intimidated by one's environment or working with, learning from, and creating with others. Building a Drive to Thrive is about allowing yourself and everyone in your organization to gain the information, insights, and inspiration needed to address and overcome the list of "lack of"s with which you are faced. In the last trait, we spoke about overcoming versus being overcome. Building a Drive to Thrive is the next step, putting it all into bigger-picture action. Once you've identified your "lack of"s and made the decision to overcome them (rather than being overcome by them), it's time to pop the machine into drive and create a collaborative plan for thriving as a collective whole in the long term.

The Unification of the Organization

When my hockey-playing days ended years ago, I craved another outlet—something that could provide the challenge and the adrenaline rush that playing hockey did for me. That passion became drumming, which evolved into my playing in a band and developing a real passion for researching and learning about drums. Over the past twenty years of drumming, I have become very loyal to one particular company because of the legendary quality, craftsmanship, and tonal characteristics that their drums provide. That company is Yamaha. My experiences playing with, researching, and learning from Yamaha drum experts led me to realize that the quality of these drums and their distinctive tonal characteristics is a direct result of the quality of the people building them and the organization that inspires them to be better, to do better, and to make better drums. As I have been told repeatedly by drum shop owners who have visited the factories located in Japan and China, the company provides opportunities for employees to refine and share their knowledge, which in some cases, has been handed down from past generations. Dave, a five-star drum shop owner in Toronto once told me that, on a trip to one of the factories, he saw firsthand just how much pride the workers took in their craft. It seemed like they approached their craft as if every drum kit that was being built was a 'special order' item! I was told by drum shop owner Angelo, who has traveled many times to the Yamaha factories in Japan, that one way this company has achieved this level of success is by valuing and allowing collaboration between workers and others outside of the organization: the drummers and business owners who actually play and sell their instruments.

Having met and spoken with many professional drummers, drum shop owners, and sound engineers, I discovered that all agree that Yamaha drums are some of the best drums you can buy. I believe that Yamaha's ability to capture, preserve, and allow the passage of generational knowledge and a professional imperative has been a huge part of their drum-building success. They have taken the time to consult, value, and better understand the people who matter: those who use and pay for the products and services being offered, and those who build them. There is much insight that can be gained from this company. As an organization, they have learned to *inspire* and to learn from one another. They have also learned to *inquire.* These traits are essential to building a collective Drive to Thrive.

Today, the business battleground you have been forced into requires a psychosocially responsive and keenly aware approach as you build with your team a goal-driven, organizational mandate where a mutual vision and respect enable the powerful weapon of collaboration to be successfully readied when needed. Because of this, it's important to more fully address the notion of collaboration as an essential ingredient in your organization's not-so-secret recipe book for success. The fact is, too often collaboration is confused with cooperation.

During my doctoral studies at Lancaster University, I had the opportunity to meet and attend a lecture given by a very influential academic scholar named Etienne Wenger-Trayner. I recall sitting patiently in the lecture hall, waiting for the presentation to begin and vowing that when I got to his level, I would give my presentations a rock concert feel! As the pioneer of the concept of community of practice, Wenger-Trayner greatly inspired me. His work has very much influenced my own thinking, work, and research. The concept of community of practice is essentially built around the somewhat messy notion of collaboration. As a leader, you can benefit from understanding this concept, which embraces and calls for a united vision and the establishment of a collective knowledge base and inspired form of work.

Within your organization, there will be some tasks that demand coordination, some that demand cooperation, and some that demand collaboration. Oftentimes what is believed to be collaboration may, in fact, be cooperation, or coordination in action. Coordination is defined by a simple need to understand who needs to do what and by when. With cooperation, there is a sense of a shared mutual trust and respect between the workers and an acknowledged benefit of working together. The notion of cooperation can be an imposter for collaboration, as it has all of the hallmarks of collaboration, albeit with a few important omissions that often go undetected. In essence, cooperation is the distant cousin of collaboration, and while they may share the same DNA, when you see them side by side, they look very different!

What's unique about collaboration is that it encompasses a greater sense of urgency and commitment than does cooperation, and it is regarded by scholars like Wenger as a much more dynamic process that includes the must-have notion of belonging to a team with a shared and inspired purpose. Collaboration in its truest form includes complementary and diverse knowledge and skill sets that are supplied by people who are intellectually agile. The result of collaboration can be co-creation and innovation—the result of combining complimentary skill sets and knowledge sets, which may not intentionally take place during a cooperative endeavor. While it may sound idyllic, and achieving levels of collaboration in its truest form is no easy feat, it is achievable. It begins with putting in place the right strategies and *drive* within your organization.

I have personally witnessed how having a driving Mandate to Be Great readily enables collaboration. Remember, collaboration is distinguished from cooperation by having larger quantities of the essential ingredients that operating by the mandate provides: a sense of belonging, trust, respect, open communication, a shared vision, and intellectual agility. Having witnessed firsthand professionals operating in a work environment where these key ingredients were part of the organization's recipe for success, I have also gotten to witness collaboration at work. How did I know it was collaboration? Because I saw the creativity and innovation embedded in the daily practices and routine operations of the agency. Trait 1 (A Mandate to Be Great) fosters Trait 4 (Build a Drive to Thrive), though things do not simply start working from that point. Your organization and its people have to be taught how to *collaborate* in the truest sense of the word. The idyllic persona of collaboration fools many, so it is essential that in addition to having a professional imperative, you understand what true collaboration looks and feels like, and how to implement it. It is not always a simple science, but once mastered, it will give you the Drive to Thrive that you seek to have flowing throughout your organization.

I believe that famous American psychological researcher Bruce Tuckman was ahead of the times in his thinking and his research. In 1965, his pioneering work in the field of group dynamics alerted us to the challenges confronting people and organizations looking for a pathway to higher levels of organizational efficiency and proficiency via the process of collaborative endeavors. Tuckman developed the four stages of group development, which debunked the notion that collaboration is something warm and fuzzy:

1. Forming
2. Storming
3. Norming
4. Performing

These four easy-to-understand stages may be best remembered for the candid and accurate portrayal of the collaborative process as something that fit better into the combative realm—that is, until the group's task and vision becomes clearer, mutually shared, committed to, and built upon working relationships where mutual respect has been gained. Tuckman called the second of his four stages the "Storming" stage. During this period of the team-building process, individuals more or less jockey for position and assert themselves, attempting to gain the respect of others and a level of authority within the group. It is during this stage when the order of governance is being chiseled out that things may become heated and egos may get bruised. Although Tuckman notes not all groups may choose to take on the messy side of the collaboration-building process, the fact is, for those who do, the result can be a shared vision and a wholly committed group. The cost of taking the time to sort and "storm" things out together until you have a platform of mutual trust and respect to build upon is worth it; however, this process is not for every individual and organization.

It is no secret that many major tech companies need and value the collaboration that can take place in an office-centric, face-to-face work environment. With millions of dollars having been poured into office furnishings, decor, and amenities, companies like Google have created environments that employees don't want to leave. Recognizing the need for face-to-face collaboration, Facebook leaders are considering enacting a pay grid that rewards employees who work from the office and compensates at a different, lesser pay level those who work from home. During my tour of the Boston headquarters for Google, I recall noticing there was always a whiteboard or some form of technology never far away from where employees were hanging out. These items were strategically placed to capture the insights and creativity that can come from what I call "spontaneous collaboration" and the "cross-pollination" of workers from different divisions of the organization. Collaboration was enabled by the open-concept working environment. It didn't matter if that open space was a lunchroom or one of their spacious coffee lounges. The fact is that Google, along with other big tech companies, recognize the power of the collective mind and spirit and they intentionally structured an office setting that is determined to capture every ounce of it.

When asked to do an interactive keynote presentation on this topic for a department of a Royal Canadian Air Force base, I saw firsthand just how messy the collaboration-building process can be when the dynamic or organizational structure is distinct. At the base, the workers claimed the management could not even spell the word *collaboration,* and the management team claimed there was no one on the staff who was willing to embrace the required elements of a collaborative endeavor. In the end, most within this department wondered if collaboration was even necessary at all.

During what turned out to be a highly insightful and productive workshop, I wound up suggesting that as a twenty-first-century organization, military or not, their having the awareness, willingness, and mental agility to collaborate with one another when and where needed would be a useful tool. To better connect with the military audience, I described collaboration as being "the ultimate organizational weapon." Having served in the Canadian Armed Forces at a young age, I could appreciate the need for a hierarchical organizational structure in a military setting, and I could grasp the vocabulary and message that would hit home with them. I found myself translating all of my research-based teachings into something much more accessible to them. I spoke about the process of collaboration being one of doing the proper reconnaissance, and determining the proper target with the sights clearly focused, and a result of the primary objective of the mission achieved with precision and effectiveness. Their sniper-sharp minds latched on to the concept immediately, giving them the intrigue and fuel to begin finding their way to a greater collective mission and taking steps toward a cooperative understanding and execution of collaboration.

This unique example demonstrates the need to see each organization for its unique circumstances and challenges, and position your plan for building collaboration accordingly. Your people and culture are like no other, and it's important to speak the language of your people when building the awareness and achievement of true collaboration, along with a collective Drive to Thrive. The fact is, the top-down, hierarchical, chain-of-command-driven work environment that is necessary within a military organization is not likely the approach your business needs, especially if it would stymie the collaboration that is essential for overcoming, and not being overcome, by the challenges you face, and sourcing all of the innovative ideas you need to thrive going forward.

Where collaboration is required, building a collaborative group dynamic must be intentionally driven, and opportunities for it to develop within your agency must be scripted, at least initially. Detail out your Drive to Thrive. You can do this by having regular team-building sessions and ensuring employees in your organization get to be heard instead of always having to just listen. It is interesting that the individuals I interviewed in my research regularly cited the feeling of respect as being a key source of inspiration for them. When I dug deeper, the feeling of respect was often the result of their feeling like leaders who others in the organization valued, cared about, and listened to. Talk about a cost-effective way for you to immediately infuse a sense of belonging and commitment to your organization! I know you have the ability to listen and to value the thoughts and ideas of your team. The question is, Knowing this, why wouldn't you?

When Four Worlds Collide

In today's new world, your organization's community of practice must be able to combine what were once disconnected and distinctive online and offline realities into one unified business reality. Your new unified organizational reality means there should never be a collision for your employees as they move between the four office worlds:

1. Online
2. Offline
3. Home-based work
4. Office-based work

No longer is there an "online/offline culture." Your working worlds previously separated by time and space must now be unified. The unification of your organization requires a shift in thinking and a change in your business practice. Now is the time for you to embrace the elements of Trait 4 and Build a Drive to Thrive. Think of it as a four-lane superhighway! The four lanes, now merged, should be smooth and wide, allowing for fast, efficient travel. There should be places for people to pull over when they are tired and need to "refuel." You should be able to get where you want to go safely and quickly, without traffic jams or stoppages along the way. The destination should be clear and the route there equally so.

Building a collective Drive to Thrive in this new working world means creating one seamless reality from what may have previously been seen as four distinct office worlds. This new highway should be built to leave your employees feeling and being competent, connected, efficient, and proficient. It should afford them the ability to collaborate, to be inspired, and to find the information required in a timely manner at any time and from any space and place. This may sound like a daunting task, but if you have been paying close attention while reading this book, you should realize you have everything you need to get the job done and you are never alone.

The information and the inspiration you need is all around you in the form of your team. As you will learn in the upcoming Trait 5, Create a Kingdom of FREEdom, Techno-Resilient people and leaders regularly tap into the free expertise and insight that employees sometimes keep hidden from one another. This is true for technological insights as much as psychological or collaborative ones. An interesting observation from my research and working experiences is that the organizational leaders who get the most from their team are the ones *who give the most*. Giving is often equated with money, but in this case, it has nothing to do with it. What I discovered is that those leaders who simply led by being out in front of the desk, as opposed to remaining seated behind it, had the most impact on their employees. Again, true leaders lead and are ultimately judged by those in their organization on their day-to-day interactions, reactions, and inaction. You are judged on what you do, not what you say. When there is a disconnect between your words and your daily actions, you create a psychological divide between you and your team. You are at the heart of "keeping the Drive to Thrive alive!" The simple solution is to connect with your team by having a regular, positive, and responsive presence within your organization. It is that simple and that cost-effective.

The Impact of Glocalization

Although it's challenging, business communities can replicate levels of in-office collaboration virtually. The catch is that it can be very difficult to replicate something that is largely misunderstood, especially without the proper training and technologies in place to do it. This is what Techno-Resiliency and the Mandate to Be Great are all about. And there couldn't be a better time for anyone to embark on this journey. Out of desperation can come innovation and collaboration, and almost every leader has felt moments of desperation during or following the 2020 pandemic and the subsequent global shift in business.

Danish scholars Thomas Ryberg and Malene Charlotte Larsen from Aalborg University's Department of Communication and Psychology discovered that it may be useful for you to understand the concept of networked individualism, along with the concept of community of practice, as you begin to put a mental framework in place for how to best conceptualize, structure, or accelerate the pathway to harness the power of online collaboration that can more fully unify your organization amid these days of home work.

While the concept of community of practice emphasizes the need for very strong emotional ties that is framed by a unified organization, vision, and cooperate mandate, Ryberg and Larson emphasize the need to understand the individual and the fact that a network is a group of loose connections. This is different from the tight connections found and required in a community of practice. The term *networked individualism* reflects the contradiction noted at the beginning of this chapter; we have never been more mutually reliant on one another, yet, in the minds of these scholars, there is an intensified push toward individualization and stylized levels of personalization taking place within our society, both online and offline. The need for individualism is juxtaposed with the need, in a networked world, to be dependent on and connected to one another. This is another factor to take into account when building collaboration and your collective Drive to Thrive. The distinction between online culture and offline culture may be problematic for you. Understanding it better may be the secret ingredient for enabling higher levels of virtual collaboration in an organization that thrives.

As these scholars suggest, there can be no more distinction between online culture and office culture. We cannot view online culture as something that is disconnected from real-life activities. As Canadian scholar and author Barry Wellman notes, we are now *glocalized*—connected locally to neighbors and friends, and connected globally to others around the world. What this means for you and your organization is that online work is now office work. There is no longer a divide between online and offline realities. This is the reality of our new world, and it requires that you and every other leader develop the structures, protocols and systems that enable the required collaboration, connection, relationship building, and establishment of the shared and fluid business practice now demanded of and for your organization.

Recognizing a networked environment in which people learn, work, and play can be made up of many "loose" or what I regard as "fleeting" connections is counterbalanced by the insight your organization's community of practice requires tighter and a more committed vision and purpose. The problem with networked individualism is that it shares a loose connection with self-determination. In your new unified working work, the aim is to establish a professional imperative that views the working self differently, as something more selfless.

As a Techno-Resilient person and organization, you can achieve the characteristics and practices highlighted throughout this chapter by embracing and enacting the following skills, processes, and insights. Together, they pave the way for enabling higher levels of collaboration, the establishment of a community of practice, and the building of a collective Drive to Thrive:

1. **Become goal-driven.** The Techno-Resilient people and organizations I studied over many years were all goal-driven, both at the individual and organizational level. The goals and the mandate of each company were clearly laid out by the leader. Each employee, driven by that professional imperative, also had personal goals related to being better, doing better, and making others better. These were communicated and regularly assessed and revised. Establishing collaboration and a community of practice is heavily reliant on this undertaking.

2. **Value collaboration.** The same Techno-Resilient people and organizations also highly valued collaboration and its results. As noted previously, collaboration is a messy process that not all organizations handle well. Take time to discuss and explore the values that highlight a collaborative process in your organization. Although these values vary from one theorist to another, from my insights and research, I've learned that no leader can go wrong by espousing a

collaboration-building process that involves his/her doing the following:

    i. **Collaboratively setting organizational goals and targets.**

    ii. **Cleary communicating the organizational goals that are set, along with the leader-led greater organizational mandate.** Make sure they are clearly communicated and distributed in a multimodal manner: print, multimedia, email, signage, and, of course, interpersonal communication. Make them ubiquitous!

3. **Enable the use of technological tools that foster collaboration.** A Techno-Resilient organization provides tools that allow employees to share not just information, but also insight and inspiration from anywhere. There is a virtual space for reliable, credible, and timely information, where organizational successes, achievements, and insights can be shared. Here, insight and inspiration can be fused, and this platform can become your organizational source of pride, one that melds your four working worlds together. With some technical guidance, creativity, and vision, you can have a fast lane to refueling and building a collaborative organization with a collective Drive to Thrive.

The Art of Spontaneous Collaboration

In this chapter, we've discussed much about the strategy behind creating collaboration in your organization. However, organizations with true Techno-Resilience also recognize the need for *spontaneous* collaboration! The concept of spontaneous collaboration is highly valued and intentionally enabled in many large office-centric work-places, such as Google and Facebook, and it is something that you need to be able to replicate online. If the goal is to unify your work worlds and to seamlessly connect them, only allowing your team the opportunity to serendipitously slip into sharing deep insights in an office-centric environment is debilitating for your organization. You need the power of the collective mind in the form of collaboration to be part of your global unification process.

The days of a disconnected and disjointed working reality are over. You need your working and learning world to be unified. Accomplishing this virtually begins with creating a virtual Share Hub or Share and Care Hub designed to allow access to more than just information. You enable and creatively construct this within your organization's VPN or by using an amalgam of Facebook, Twitter, and/or Instagram. You can design a unique virtual space where employees can go to connect through a hub that offers the look, feel, and functionality that so many in this world are now are accustomed to experiencing on social media.

When it comes to actually understanding and designing a technology-based platform with hardware and software components, this is something best constructed and imagined by individuals who understand the logistics of this undertaking. What you need to know is that a Share Hub has the capacity and the functionality to do more than connect your organization's people to information. It must be capable of so much more! Many times, the information pathways that are created are narrow and unidirectional. You need information superhighways in your organization that allow people to pull over when tired and refuel at an inspiration station. You also need your information superhighway to run like the German autobahn, where there are no limits placed on how fast you can get somewhere.

When you construct the information and knowledge pathways to be wide open and multidirectional, you reduce the chances of breakdown and collision. This will assist you in more rapidly expanding the confidence and ability within your organization to virtually connect and share knowledge, inspiration, and information. The Share Hub should also allow opportunities for employees to experience spontaneous collaboration with others in the organization, as well as access to sources of inspiration in the form of organizational successes and accomplishments. In such a setting, employees have the ongoing ability and opportunity to unite, converse, inspire, create, innovate, and feel competent at what they do, at any time and from any place. They realize the ability to do this seamlessly within an organization, whether it be online, offline, from an office-centric working space, or from a home-based workstation. They are maximizing and thriving on the four-lane superhighway, and their doing so becomes vital to the organization's success.

Enabling multimodal formats for allowing your employees to share their knowledge can also involve innovative new creations, such as podcasts, videos, and multimedia presentations, which can serve to enliven, invigorate, and inspire the organization. Perhaps there can be a company podcast to which organizational leaders and stakeholders are invited to share information and insights specific to your own company, while allowing your team to inspire and inquire! You may have a leader who is not confident in presenting in a face-to-face format. However, your realizing their proficiency in another area and assigning them to host a podcast series for your organization may be the very thing that elevates this individual to a position of excellence in the organization.

I recall a fascinating story Etienne Wenger-Trayner shared about the notion of collaboration and his concept of community of practice. Early in his pioneering days, he began working with engineering firms that at the time tended to be very compartmentalized. What he was referring to was the fact that information and knowledge was being defined and confined to individual departments. When he was able to break down the walls and allow for what I refer to as a *cross-pollination* of knowledge and insight, innovation was the result. This is not to suggest that collaboration immediately followed. As you now know, there was likely much work to be done in enabling and teaching that process throughout the organization. However, according to Etienne Wenger-Trayner, allowing for the sharing and the co-construction of knowledge across and among departments previously operating in isolation was a vital organizational stimulus. It is one that every leader can benefit from.

If your organization is not yet harnessing the power of the Drive to Thrive insight in this chapter, there is good news: you have already taken the first step toward achieving it by absorbing the knowledge within these pages. The process is one that begins by breaking down your organization's knowledge barriers by viewing them as another one of your "lack of"s (Trait 3). Once you do, you will have something that can be locked onto as an organizational goal. Don't view it as a barrier that can't be scaled, but rather, see the value in it as the first crucial step toward achieving collaboration. It seems simple enough; however, there were many athletes I coached who struggled with setting goals and overcoming mental hang-ups that stymied their progress. By merely valuing and understanding how and why the cross-pollination of knowledge within your organization must be unified and setting an organizational goal to achieve this, you are well on your way to thriving.

If unifying your working world into something that can better capture the collective organizational knowledge, insights, and inspiration that fuels the Mandate to Be Great in your employees is something you value, you need to see it as a short-term "lack of," and then make it an organizational goal as something to overcome together. Combine these insights by creating online spaces and places that do more than just supply a one-way street of information in the manner previously noted, and you will have a way to provide your organization with something more at a time when it seems like there is so much less being offered and received.

Establishing a community of practice within an organization recognizes the need to break down any knowledge barriers that may exist between team members and departments. In doing so, you cultivate a much deeper *shared* vision and purpose. When you bring that onto the organizational playing field, you can rapidly change the score in your favor very quickly! Demonstrating and replicating the desire to be better, do better, and make others better (the Mandate to Be Great) in more than just a few people in your organization is a natural by-product when you unify your organizational world. It also opens up the organization to more quickly expand pockets of resilience.

A Mandate Minute

A Techno-Resilient organization in the new world in which we live can't afford to distinguish and operate as online and offline. Your organizational worlds have now collided and online, offline, office-centric, and home-based work need to become one connected working world. Building one world where information and inspiration can rapidly flow is enabled by a technological infrastructure that is built on understanding the need for, the value in, and the true nature and power of collaboration.

Trait 5
CREATE A KINGDOM
OF FREEDOM

The content of this entire book has been challenging you and your organization to be guided by something much more than just fear- or risk-management. *Mandate to Be Great* is a proactive approach and movement toward leading an organization that is premised on the desire to be better, to do better, and to make those in your organization better. It is fueled by passion and a guiding Techno-Resilient spirit. With this in mind, you want to be using that Techno-Resilient spirit and mindset to guide your decisions around the purchasing of new technologies for your organization. It's time to demand something more than the bells-and-whistles sales pitches than can be found on every virtual corner. When you've created a free-flowing, highly productive organizational highway, every stop you make to refuel or add value should be strategically thought out. In Trait 5, Create a Kingdom of FREEdom, you will come to realize that you can "make something from nothing" when you realize how much you actually have surrounding you.

In a world that is shifting at a more rapid pace than many of us have seen, people are *very* willing to sell you "what you need."

This limited form of training is that which only touches the surface of skill building and does not get to the heart of what your team needs to know. Many technology-vendor demonstrations advertise this type of bells-and-whistles professional development as what your organization needs to survive and thrive going forward in a technology-enhanced or technology-driven environment. Their sales pitches may highlight gimmicky aspects of the product, whose luster and shine may have limited curb appeal or longevity. They may catch your attention initially, but then cause you to begin to more deeply question what your team truly needs.

When so many are attempting to sell you on the "next best" technology or professional development, and marketing proclaims that every organization should keep pace with the latest versions of everything, it is important to stay mindful and know where your power lies. You need to move beyond the loud echoes of any bells-and-whistles sales pitches and dig deeper. Trait 5 of Techno-Resilient people and organizations is about Creating a Kingdom of FREEdom by looking for, asking for, and seizing all available cost-effective and cost-saving opportunities within and outside of your organization.

I may be the originator of the concept of Techno-Resilience, but I would never advocate "techno-lust," the unnecessary and mis-guided purchasing and use of technology in teaching, in the work-place, or for personal use. Technology for the sake of technology is an expensive and ill-advised trap that your organization can become caught up in. In our new world where finances are tight, you need to make informed and prudent decisions about how you will in-vest the money you've designated for advancing your technological infrastructure and training. I have always advocated an "If it ain't broke, don't fix it" mentality. This does not mean you shouldn't always be on the lookout for new ways of becoming increasingly

Techno-Resilient and Techno-Efficient. What it *does* means is that you don't want to invest in the latest and the greatest technology simply because it is "the thing to do." Do it because it makes sense for you and your team, not because everyone else is doing it. There is no right way, only a right way for you, right now. You are best guided by a Techno-Resilient mindset that invests time to explore a technology before spending. Make vendors accountable, and avoid the bells-and-whistles professional development. What really matters in this new technology-enhanced world is how this technology will improve your organizational workflow and your ability to be more Techno-Efficient.

When you seek to create systems that support your *know where*, ask yourself, Is it a technology my team can and will use, and will it be worth the investment? Will my team feel and be more effective as a result of the technology? Is it really an upgrade? In your quest for true Techno-Resiliency and Techno-Efficiency, you must be guided by the following questions: Will this technology improve on what we are currently doing? Will it lead to a higher level of Techno-Efficiency within our organization? If what you have and what you are doing is currently getting the job done, why invest the money? Perhaps you are better off investing your time and energy into developing a hard skill set and a Techno-Resilient mindset within your organization that will last far longer and provide intangibles that no piece of hardware or software could ever provide.

In my research and observations of Techno-Resilient organizations that were working with limited finances and resources, I found that they had to be more diligent in their research and decision-making. When cash is tight, it calls for more might. It's time to flex that Techno-Resilience muscle. Techno-Resilient people and organizations leave no stone unturned. They make use of all available resources, most notably, free in-house PD (personal/

professional development). They make sure the skills and talents of employees are being best utilized and fully tapped into. Techno-Resilient people and organizations also realize older technologies are not necessarily bad. Instead, they are guided by standards and answers to questions that help them determine when, why, and how to upgrade so that they can avoid the trappings of "techno-lust," the unnecessary and uniformed purchasing of a latest technology. This is a fundamental operating principle for those regarded as truly Techno-Resilient. They know to let their mandate guide them, not external marketing.

Ask the Right Questions

After having developed the first networked computer lab in our school district during my first teaching job in the public school system, I was told the following year that all computers had to be "locked down" and I would be losing my network administrator privileges. From that point on, a newly established tech support department would be governing everything from a distance. Having been my own IT department and having essentially established a point of pride for our organization in the form of a fully networked computer lab (not to mention a virtual learning hub/Share Hub for students with a totally unique information technology curriculum), I was being left handcuffed. The newly appointed IT leader in our school district failed to recognize the balance between security, productivity, and accessibility. He was let go a short time later, and we were faced with rebuilding our previous momentum. The lock-down mentality had taken over as the mandate for governing the fast-emerging PC-based computer labs springing up all over, and it was stifling access and enthusiasm for educators and students alike.

This was at a time when expectations, curiosity, and excitement levels were high, as computers with an internet connection offered a promise of hope for a new and inspired way to enhance learning and teaching.

This type of unfortunate situation arises because it alerts you to the fact that Techno-Resilient people and organizations are guided by (and need to be guided by) something more than a lockdown mentality when it comes to technology use. They need freedom—freedom to create, to innovate, to decide, to recalibrate, and to rethink older technologies, etc. There is a recognition of the need to balance accessibility with cybersecurity, all in a bid to enhance and support productivity and organizational efficiency. Lean toward technologies that support the overall enhancement of the organization's ability to get the job done!

It is amazing how easily one can lose sight of this point. I experienced an example of this just recently when I was involved in a strategic planning meeting for the board of directors on which I sit. The facilitator of the session was using Zoom to virtually connect our team. We ended up going into Zoom breakout rooms for more focused discussions. This was effortlessly and seamlessly facilitated by the Zoom platform. Many of our board members lamented the fact our current platform does not allow for this and the fact that what we are currently using is so much more cumbersome. The tightened cybersecurity offered by the previous platform we'd used for our board meetings had taken precedence over features that enabled functionality and collaboration. You must carefully and strategically balance the equation based on your reality and needs. Just remember, good decision-making is enabled by a process of exercising due diligence and asking the right questions.

While working with an educational technology leader, I once proposed an "action research" project whereby we negotiated with the vendor a three-month exploration period with the technology in question. During that time, I worked with the team to get insights into what they liked and disliked about the technology and, ultimately, whether they thought it would be worth the investment. After the three-month investigation, I presented a report with the entire organizational team that was based on our collective reflections, explorations, and findings. Aside from being a very powerful and insightful tool for making informed technological purchases, it also acted as an exercise in demonstrating the power of collaboration and what a desire to do better and be better as an organization entails. I am a big advocate of this type of action research taking place within organizations prior to the sizeable purchase of new technologies and building the systems and platforms for your *know where.*

One of the best ways to avoid the traps of costly, unnecessary, or unsuitable technologies is to ensure you ask the right questions of product vendors and your IT team members. Ask the wrong questions, and you'll get the wrong answers. Consider asking deeper questions that will help better inform your purchases and determine their worthiness.

In light of the fact that there are many available technologies and applications you and your organization may be considering, the following are some general guiding questions to which you should be getting answers:

1. **Does the technology heighten and easily allow for collaborative work practices?** As I noted in Trait 4, this is a vital question and consideration for your team. With home work becoming the new norm, you need information to be seamlessly shared across platforms and networks. Anything less will stymie proficiency and efficiency. Establishing a true community of practice requires the breaking down of

departments in a way that allows for the cross-pollination of information and inspiration. Most software and hardware developers today are cognizant of this new reality, and they should be able to articulate and support this level of functionality.

2. **Where is the technology on the cybersecurity/accessibility scale?** A technology that is designed and governed by a lockdown mentality can be frustrating for employees and stymie the productivity and user-friendliness you need for your team. When you have employees working from home, often acting as their own IT department, you can't afford for them to be wasting precious time and energy trying to access a system. Be sure you thoroughly research this important point. In the twenty-first century, cybersecurity is a must for your organization; however, it must also be meticulously weighed against and balanced with your goals and the ambitions for the technology.

3. **Are you able to have a free trial period?** Can you access the technology for free and allow your team members to explore and examine how the technology fits into their daily work practice? Follow the same framework I did while conducting the action research investigation for which we were granted a three-month trial with the technology before any actual purchase was made. Work with your team and thoroughly investigate the technology together. See it in action before deciding whether or not to purchase it.

Techno-Resilient people and organizations are not afraid to ask for more, explore more, and demand more from their technology purchases and vendors. With so many cost-effective technologies now available, don't be afraid to ask for free trial periods and training before making costly technology purchases. Adopting, adapting, and enacting a Techno-Resilient positive growth mindset involves *getting involved*. Be proactive, not passive. Being actively engaged in the process of choosing technologies that, in some cases, can have a revolutionary impact upon your organization's ability to collaborate and ultimately enhance productivity is actually an exciting endeavor for your team. Don't take these purchases lightly. However, also realize that sometimes older technologies still have the power to get the job done within your organization!

Bricolage: The Art of Making Do, Even If It's Not New

Creating an organizational Kingdom of FREEdom begins by regularly making principled and cost-effective purchases that add value and efficiency to your daily operations. Looking for all available resources within and outside of your agency also involves taking advantage of free training opportunities when they are offered and becoming innovative with existing technologies. This Techno-Resiliency trait means being resourceful and cost-effective. When freeing up resources and expenses, you also mentally free up your organization with the comforting knowledge that you are now guided by something more than "techno-lust." You are guided by principles that can only positively impact the decisions you and your team make.

There is a story that has gained some notoriety over the years. I often tell it when I share examples of how I was Techno-Resilient in my quest to build a networked computer lab all those years ago. It serves as a true testament to what is possible when your desire to make something happen exceeds the resources that are available to you. As the story goes, attempting to build a computer lab with no computers or funding is a daunting task at best; however, I was informed there were many old computers that had been thrown into a dumpster by a local business. After getting permission from them to take a dumpster dive, I found myself literally rummaging through a dumpster to salvage whatever I could to build my lab! Near the top there was a rather large laser printer perched among some other broken computer parts. I had no idea if it worked, but more than twenty years ago, a laser printer was all the rage, and I had to have one. The fact of the matter is, when I got it back to the lab, I discovered there were two serial ports on the back (nothing was USB at this time). Long story short, the first port did not work, but with a new cable, the second port worked fine. This laser printer served as our school's main printer for three years before funding was allocated to purchase a newer model. Even then, the "dumpster dive laser printer," as it was known, was still used as an important and useful backup.

During my immersive observation period in the organizations I researched, one of the key Techno-Resilient strategies and positive growth mindsets I observed in action was the understanding by the leadership team and employees that older technologies still have value, and that making efficient use of whatever was available to them to get the job done was a natural response for them. In one example of this, I noticed a pod of much older PCs strategically placed in an open area. I often witnessed students and teachers from different classes regularly coming and going from this pod of computers that would have most surely been dismissed as nonfunctional by most. When I dug deeper, I discovered these relics had been scaled back to a bare-bones operating system and were equipped with word processing software only. All of the computers were attached through a dated "switch box"-type mechanism to an equally dated printer. This hub of dinosaurs was serving as an effective word processing station for students and educators alike.

In order for this to occur, someone had to be motivated to find value in what was around them in a bid to be better, do better, and make those around them better. While many would have been quick to dismiss as valueless the outdated technologies that were being used, I was told in an interview that the professional who made this happen came in on a weekend and was determined to make IT happen because there was a need for it.

There is a wonderful term that captures the essence of this practice: *bricolage,* which we first explored in Trait 3. Bricolage is the construction of something from anything that's available. To me, this term is a close cousin to the concept of resilience, as both share the inherent characteristics of inner strength and adaptability. To make use of all available resources and construct something from them requires imagination, creativity, resourcefulness, and determination. Those whom I observed making resilient and inspired use of technology with limited resources and available technologies in their workplace were guided by something more. They were also most assuredly and collectively guided by a Mandate to Be Great.

In an excerpt taken from one of my Techno-Resiliency research interviews, Steve was suffering from rural isolation and the fact that internet access was still largely hit-and-miss within his office building. He could have made excuses, but instead, the Techno-Resilient spirit, growth mindset and practices within this organization exemplified the notion of bricolage to its fullest! Rather than dismissing as valueless the older resources they had access to, his organization found value in them and what they did. Steve identified a common concern faced by many organizations: the constant struggle to keep up with the techno Joneses. He said, "I think trying to find the perfect recipe to improve [office] management, to improve the [overall] experience, to be progressive, to be current, yes, that requires a lot of resiliency. I mean, things change so fast. They often say, 'You're never going to get there, no matter what technology you're using or what platform you're using. You're never going to get there. You're never going to master any of them because the technology changes so fast.' So, I think the value comes in being resourceful, adaptable, and learning how to make use of available technologies, whatever the current flavor is."

Steve was right. His spirit was one of truly Creating a Kingdom of FREEdom by making innovation a close ally.

Keeping It In-House

When it comes to Trait 5 of Techno-Resilient people and organizations, one very noticeable practice I observed in my research was how the Techno-Resilient used in-house professional development. This means tapping into the expertise of your team members and enabling them to confidently share it with others. This is a practice that adds tremendous value to your organization. Recognize the talents and proficiencies of your team, your people. It's something that is sitting right in front of you, and it is so often overlooked. Many team members carry around hidden talents and insights that are just waiting to be unlocked. Part of that unlocking process involves building a working environment where individuals feel comfortable and valued. It was very obvious to me that in the organizations I studied, sharing and caring permeated the workplace. On any given day, I would witness employees confidently leading workshops and impromptu teaching sessions with others. There was a level of assuredness and autonomy within the organization, granted by each team leader and by the employees, that collectively they had enough knowledge and determination to *make IT happen,* in spite of any perceived "lack of"s.

You may already have in-house the information, strategies, systems, or insights you need. If you don't, your people may very well know where to find them! Utilizing in-house PD in the way I observed through my research needs to be taking place within your organization. Tapping into the knowledge wealth that exists within your company means you are tapping into a global market of information, as your employees are indeed "glocalized" through their access to the online information superhighway.

Inspiring and building confidence in your team members to share what they know can also be enabled by realizing there are many formats for sharing and presenting information. Traditionally, the office-centric, PowerPoint-driven, group presentation format has dominated, though it is not for everyone. Find multimodal ways for your people to share and communicate what they know. Make use of and maximize new portals likes Share Hubs. The Share Hub that you create for your organization will become an easy and effective starting place for your people to get comfortable with sharing work-related knowledge and insights. There, they can also collaboratively discuss and decide on potential new or old technologies that can support growth efforts and the greater collective mandate.

As you move forward to enact Trait 5 in this manner, if you really want to build the confidence in your team to take the next steps in presenting and sharing what they know, be sure to acknowledge and comment on content that is posted in something like a Share Hub. Be active and be involved as a leader. We live in a "how many likes" society, where people gain confidence by seeing their number of likes go up. However, you need to think beyond the likes mentality that governs us and leave a comment explaining what you actually like about a particular insight or piece of information that has been shared. If you don't happen to like something that has been shared, be honest, open, and fair in your critique.

Your team can benefit from a differentiated approach in terms of how they share and learn the information they need. It is another aspect of becoming a twenty-first-century Techno-Resilient organization. However, the underlying and predominant aspect of Creating a Kingdom of FREEdom is a belief in your people and in what they bring to the table to get the job done. It's about knowing that you have what it takes to create or access the resources—technological, systematic, or psychological—to move forward. When you embrace the elements of a Techno-Resilient organization, you equip yourself and your team with a positive growth mindset and a simple decision-making process that leads to decisive and informed assessments that you and your team can live with going forward in a world that all too often can feel like it has been set one step backward.

A Mandate Minute

Debunking the notion that "Nothing in life is free," Creating your Kingdom of FREEdom is built on your determination to get the most out of what you have at your disposal—what is sitting right in front of you! Making something from nothing occurs when you realize how much you actually have in the people that make up your organization. Encouraging a positive growth mindset that is focused on making efficient use of all people, materials, and knowledge-based resources is guided by asking the right questions. In this new world, the questions that need to be asked have changed considerably. At a time when asking yesterday's questions will get you the wrong answers for today's world, the important questions for you to ask yourself are, Am I asking the right questions for my organization? and Am I getting the most from everything I already have?

Mastering Techno-Efficiency

I n order to do better, you must know better. And now you do! Having read this book, you should be able to see the big picture for your organization that is intricately framed by a Mandate to Be Great, with the main subject of the portrait being the people in your organization and your collaboration around a central goal, vision, or objective. Creating a movement from your mandate all begins with your people. Illuminate them as something much more than abstract images within your organization, as they are the main stars of this show.

Today and every day, it is your people, not your products, profits, or promotions, that must be painted in bold, bright, and beautiful Techno-Resilient colors. It is your people who will help you not only to master the art and science of becoming Techno-Resilient (cultivating your capacity for thriving as a technology-enhanced workplace by maximizing existing resources and team efficiencies while minimizing costs and new-world complexities), but also to move forward to the point of becoming a truly Techno-Efficient organization.

Techno-Efficiency is an organizational mastery of the ability to do more with less support in a technology-mediated workspace. It is a phenomenon I observed during my research, and it is fueled at the individual level by a Techno-Resilient growth mindset that pushes an individual beyond the realm of being merely self-determined into what you now recognize as something governed more by the collective and collaborative spirit found within the Mandate to Be Great. Being Techno-Efficient not only refers to the ability to harness the power of whatever technologies are available at the time, it also denotes an ability and skill set that push an individual to willingly and effectively, and in a timely manner, make use of all available information and resources. To be Techno-Efficient at the highest level, you must be equipped with a mindset that is prepared to embrace problem-solving as a natural part of a technology-enhanced work environment.

Techno-Efficient individuals recognize the need to maximize the use of time. In order to accomplish this, they have developed, out of necessity, what I call *informal coping frameworks* for overcoming the "lack of"s in the office, as well as *informal collective frameworks* for overcoming. My research and work propose these can and should be made into something more formalized. I have unpacked, repackaged, and labeled the highly efficient practices I've observed at work in other individuals and organizations and presented them to you in the form of a Mandate to Be Great.

The ability to reframe your organization in this new world, with a guiding mandate and ultimate associated efficiencies, involves a big picture that is much more than just a vision frantically framed by extraordinarily challenging times. It is an opportunity to rise to clarity, and to come together to ride the seismically shifting tides squared in the direction of a new Mandate to Be Great. It is one that you, your people, and your organization will collaboratively create and can be collectively inspired by. The picture that will be painted will be a clearly focused depiction of what organizational life (with the emphasis on "life"!) can be. It will be the living, breathing organism created from the maximization of your organizational metabolism.

What you create from here can be your real-life depiction of an action scene, with you in the director's chair. Your work and direction can ultimately lead to true Techno-Efficiency, or it can lead to your getting stuck in a continuous search for answers and a way around perceived barriers and "lack of"s. The power that can be harnessed and that can flow through your organization with an inspired employee base—one that is regularly supported and mentored on how to be better, do better, and make those around them better—is one that is fueled and ignited by you. From this point forward, you can choose to be the action-oriented superhero who inspires the superhero within each and every one of your employees! This is your role to embrace, and now, equipped with the new powers you have discovered within these pages, you are properly outfitted to take on this calling and conquer some of the biggest challenges facing you in this new world of home work, "lack of"s, and financial and psychological strains the likes of which we've never known. You have the power to enable a collective growth mindset and a Techno-Resilient skill set, but no power can come from realization alone. It must be paired with an action plan. Your research-supported action plan is laid out in the 5 Traits of Techno-Resilient People and Organizations:

Trait 1:   **A Mandate to Be Great**
          Have and build within your team a driving professional imperative!

Trait 2:   **No What, No How, but You Had Better Know Where!**
          Address your "no how" with "know-how."

Trait 3:   **Barriers + Bridges = Breakthroughs**
          Find a "meta-for" moving *overcome* to *overcoming*.

Trait 4:   **Build a Drive to Thrive**
                Be in command of your mentor "ship."
Trait 5:   **Create a Kingdom of FREEdom**
                Develop a low-cost, user-friendly, internal capacity.

The Mandate to Be Great is not intended to be a piece of abstract artwork that is crafted for you to stand and look at for hours, only to walk away while still trying to interpret it. In this new world framed in a not-so-gentle fashion by bigger global circumstances, you must always remember that *inspiration is your new innovation.* Everything else is to be built upon this foundational understanding. Inspiration ignites the mandate. Inspiration is the thread that weaves the 5 Traits together and throughout your organization. This book has given you the strategies to do more with (a whole lot) less. It has given you innovative perspectives that could lead to a competitive edge, new lane, new product line, and a much more adaptive workplace. And, most important, it has provided you with the directional know-how to be better and do better, driven full force by the mandate you create with and for your team. All of this is fueled by your desire to inspire and be inspired!

In Trait 1, A Mandate to Be Great, you came to recognize the need for a psychologically and emotionally supportive workplace in the wake of the COVID-19 pandemic, one in which the mantra "people before profit" drives your policies and interactions. It helped you understand that doing this begins to inspire a deep-set professional imperative within your team that is something far greater than self-determination. It's time to put self on the shelf! We are operating in an entirely new world. Employees with a professional imperative have a desire to inspire and be inspired. They want to learn, and they are willing to share what they know. In essence, they value the benefits found in a community of practice where there are tight ties and a common drive to get the job done right, with integrity acting as a driving force.

In Trait 2, No What, No How, but You Had Better Know Where!, you discovered the twenty-first-century reality that has largely gone unnoticed by many, one that Techno-Resilient people and organizations capitalize on. The fact is, you don't have to know it all! Once you deciphered the cryptic title of Trait 2, you realized the "No What, No How, Know Where" refers to the new reality that knowing where to find the information you need in a timely manner and being able to validate and authenticate it is vital for your organization, especially with the move toward mastering the new world's working environment.

With the internet as your information superhighway, you have been alerted to the fact that your team is now more "glocalized" than ever before, constantly connected at the local level and global level. When workers are without the security and familiarity of their workplace-based community of practice, where strong ties can more easily unite, they still have opportunities to come together in similar ways. In the online, networked world, even loose ties with others can offer insight, connections, and information. Once a sense of NEThics is understood and taught to your team members, along with the Techno-Resiliency growth mindset of believing that you can thrive as a technology-enhanced workplace by seeing barriers as "lack of"s, it will morph into becoming a seasoned Techno-Efficient skill set that can carry your organization forward. You'll then have a skill set that can transition between office-centric and home-based workspaces and online and offline places. This is your mandate in action. You have added to your superpowers the ability to turn what were previously viewed as barriers into true breakthroughs, the topic of Trait 3.

Bolstering your new understanding of the power of collaboration and internet-based knowledge is the confidence you've gained from Trait 3, Barriers + Bridges = Breakthroughs. With the proper training, a Techno-Resilient growth mindset leads to a Techno-Efficient skill set. When you choose to see barriers as merely "lack of"s, it instills a sense of confidence and belief in your team. Where the notion of barriers may have placed a negative psychological judgment on your team's ability to overcome the challenges you face, viewing them as merely "lack of"s ignites the desire to unite, to set goals, and to build upon and overcome them. This is, of course, in opposition to being overcome by them. The psychological edge that comes from this belief and unique understanding is undeniable. This shift in perspective is a hallmark of the Techno-Resilient individuals and organizations I've studied. You must maximize internal capacities within your organization and recognize the talents and proficiencies of your team members, as doing so allows you to discover what is needed to crush the mental hang-up of any and all perceived barriers.

If the *desire to inspire and be inspired* is considered to be a thematic thread that has weaved its way through the 5 Traits, then the unification of the organization that comes with Trait 4, Build a Drive to Thrive, is the needle that pulls the thread through the fabric. In your now-reframed new working world, the ability to unify your mission and your vision of what you want your organization to become can be uniquely sculpted from the Mandate to Be Great. At this time, when your team has been split apart by home work, office-centric work, online work, and offline work, it could be easy to dismiss the unification of your organization as something that is impossible. The Techno-Resilient organization knows differently! The fact is, the unification of your team has never been more important and more vital to your organization's success, and it is not as difficult as your new world's circumstances may initially make it appear to be.

The blueprint for how to do this is that of creating a very strong and underlying current—the one that runs through this entire book. It is the need to unify and transform the power found in each individual within your organization into the power of the collective. If you were to put it under a microscope and zoom in all the way to full magnification, you'd see what I saw: the organizations researched were unified in their vision and their collective willingness to do whatever was needed to get the job done right. Having that collective, collaborative Drive to Thrive is much like turning the corner on turning up your Techno-Efficiency, as you have the needle fully threaded and can start sewing a pattern of greatness with vigor throughout the fabric of your team and organization.

While this book has spotlighted resilience and inspiration in a totally unique way, it has also highlighted the darker side of collaboration, alerting you to the fact that cultivating levels of collaboration within your organization is not going to be without its fair share of confrontation. The reality is, even people with a strong desire to do better, be better, and make others better are going to need to find their way through and around the multiple personalities, diverse skill sets, and job requirements that make up all organizations. Just remember, the unification of the organization will always be a challenge, but it should never be considered a barrier. If you have learned anything from how the Techno-Resilient approach their "lack of," you now have the power of the real-life insight and the research-backed plan that this book provides you with to begin your quest.

The final trait, Trait 5, Create a Kingdom of FREEdom, is about your team moving forward together and signaling that you have arrived at a destination where Techno-Efficiency is now leading the way. However, in order to enter this kingdom, you must have your people see and find the value in working with others and with whatever resources are available to them at the time. Although my grandma always told me, "Nothing in life is ever free," making something from nothing and making do with what resources you have (bricolage) seem to be exempt from grandma's scrutiny! They are also hallmarks of a Techno-Resilient spirit and a Techno-Efficient skill set.

When it comes to creating your Kingdom of FREEdom, you could add the power of an individualized VPN to your organization in the form of a Share Hub, where all of the information, inspiration, and collaboration is more easily accessed, enabled, and corralled. What's important is that you recall what was mentioned earlier: a vision is never complete; it is always growing and evolving. Just the same, Techno-Efficiency is not an end-point destination. Times will continue to change, the unexpected will continue to occur within your organization and within our bigger global society, and you, your team, and your organization will continue to grow and innovate.

It is my intention that you can take these 5 Traits and the tools therein and go forth to build a psychologically responsive workplace where you can all come together to obtain cost-effective resources, create innovative solutions for every perceived barrier, and uncover new efficiencies each and every day. I have every confidence that once you have a Drive to Thrive, have built your mandate, and know how to set things into motion, you will not only be able to restart your engine after times of great socioeconomic challenge, but also charge it to full capacity so that your ride down the highway takes you and your people to places never before experienced—to the point of creating a truly Techno-Resilient and Techno-Efficient organization.

No matter where you are today or where you are going, your organization can choose to make a date with a mandate and master their home work to become Techno-Resilient. I have witnessed professionals in organizations make do with outdated technologies and have a transformational impact on student learning and employee engagement that other organizations with newer technologies simply could not match. What it all comes down to is that there is no match for an organization that is guided by a Mandate to Be Great and all that comes with it.

In psychology, the term *stage theory* represents a series of steps or phases in a process that occur over a period of time. Some stage theories suggest you must progress through each stage before you can advance to the next. Others are discontinuous and suggest you can progress and regress through the stages in a nonlinear manner. The Mandate to Be Great possesses some of the characteristics of a stage theory in that the way individuals progress through their mastery of the 5 Traits may vary. It may not be linear or as they are presented here, based on where one's organization stands, what "lack of"s they face, or what other organizational mandates they have in place. When I enter organizations to do a Techno-Resiliency audit, I look to see where they are in terms of each of the 5 Traits. What you have in your possession with the 5 Traits is your tool kit, to be used in your own way, with the Mandate to Be Great always being the thread woven throughout each trait and the tools and strategies therein. Each of these traits is presented as a stand-alone entity. After I've interviewed members of the leadership team and a sample of selected employees, we determine where the work should begin. Some organizations may begin at Trait 1, while others may need to optimize Trait 3 to truly get their engines going. The 5 Traits are indeed stages of organizational development; however, they are nonlinear. You can start working on developing the skills and growth mindset found in Trait 5 as easily as you can begin developing Trait 1.

Early on in this book, you were alerted to the fact that enacting and achieving the Mandate to Be Great is an ongoing journey without an end point. Much like the golf swing and the game of golf itself, it is designed to be continually improved upon and evolve as old technologies undergo innovation and new technologies become available. In the game of golf you continually try to build a golf swing and a mental mindset that is able to deal with the considerable challenges you are regularly faced with on the course. There are many ways to hit the ball straight, and with newly available tools, you can increase your drive distance and decrease your drive time. However, if you know anything about the game of golf (and the stark metaphorical use of this analogy), you would know that despite all of the diversity in the way people swing the club, their styles, their height, and the way they see what lies ahead, there are basic mental and physical fundamentals to which all must adhere. The same holds true in your adaptation to and implementation of the 5 Traits and supporting Mandate to Be Great.

This is all to be said with one word of caution: you must realize that as fast as you can make progress, you can also quickly regress. Going back to the metaphor of the resilience muscle I mentioned previously, I believe your organization has a form of muscle memory, and once you start developing and strengthening your organization's Techno-Resiliency muscles by integrating and operating by the traits and strategies within this book, you will always remember what you did and what you can do! In the end, your journey to becoming Techno-Resilient and Techno-Efficient must be regarded as a *differentiated* journey in that your team's unique needs must be strategically crafted and suited to the distinctive character of your organization. Be compassionate with your unique challenges, people, and "lack of"s.

The COVID-19 pandemic has united us all in that we have overcome something extraordinary, and as we go forward, we must all find value in and capitalize on what is within our grasp. Those individuals and organizations that are able to increase levels of

Techno-Resiliency within themselves and others will have a clear-cut advantage. They are the ones who will thrive. Amid all of my research, development, and presentation of the process and the fundamentals of Techno-Resiliency, one point was imminently clear: with a spotlight on the positive aspects of organizational efficiency and the concept of resiliency itself (with a techno twist, of course), you will find yourself able to enjoy the game of business you are in and ultimately feel good about what you need to do, how you need to do it, and what the benefits will be for everyone involved.

Mandate to Be Great and what you create from and with it was designed to be a feel-good story—not with a happy *ending,* but rather, with a happy *journey.* In sharing, encouraging, and implementing the 5 Traits of Techno-Resilient People and Organizations, there should be no end to the joy and healthy challenges that can be found in building an organization where your people are supported and directed to be better, do better, and make others around them better. I have every confidence that you can maximize your internal capacity to overcome, and not be overcome by, the "lack of"s you are confronted with each and every day. In implementing all that you have read and learned within these pages, your organization can ooze with positive ambition and focus. And from there, you can experience a happy ending at the end of each workday, knowing your team is headed in the right direction, full steam ahead on the highway to Techno-Efficiency!

Are you ready to become Techno-Resilient?

To book your Techno-Resilience
audit and step into greater Techno-Efficiency,
contact Dr. Rob Graham at

rob@technoresiliency.com

or visit

technoresiliency.com

Client Testimonials

"Dr. Rob Graham is a leader in the conceptualization and practice of Techno-Resiliency. A well-regarded thinker and scholar in the educational technology space, Rob understands that our contemporary world can only go forward if we bring the ideal of Techno-Resiliency to all aspects of work, business, and life in general. He inspires those looking for a better and brighter world to learn how to leverage technology in unique and life-affirming ways. In our post-pandemic world, Rob's message could not be more important. I hope you will have the opportunity to meet and work with my colleague Rob Graham. You and those around you will be inspired and positioned for the sustained world of change we live in."

— Dr. Lorraine Carter, Director, McMaster University Continuing Education

"I have known Dr. Rob Graham for over a decade. I was studying with him at Lancaster University at a time when he was shaping his pioneering and innovative theory of Techno-Resiliency. Rob's pragmatic 'Making *IT* Happen' approach provides a unique and inspirational foundation for organizational development."

— Dr. Andy Hollyhead, PhD, MA, BSc (Hons), BA, Associate Lecturer, The Open University, Milton Keynes, UK; Former Associate Professor and Lead Academic, Governance and Assurance Hub, Birmingham City University

"Dr. Graham is a gift to any organization. His technical knowledge matches his superb teaching abilities, making Dr. Graham a welcomed instructor in any learning environment. His research skills are solid and his ideas regarding computer use are progressive and forward-thinking."

— **Dr. Jennifer Barnett, Professor, Nipissing University**

"Dr. Rob Graham's contributions to our organization have been substantial. As chair of our board's human resources committee, Rob's level of engagement has been exemplary, and he excels at keeping our committee organized, productive, and on task. By donating his time and talent to our not-for-profit, Rob has truly made a lasting impact, and we're very grateful for how much he gives back to our community."

— **Tessa Clermount, Executive Director of the North Bay Military Family Resource Centre**

"Rob's professionalism and expertise in interacting with our students are second to none. As a welcomed favorite among both coaches and students, Rob has the ability to consistently find innovative and inspiring ways to connect course material to clients young and old. His positive attitude, diverse background, and inherent skills in being relatable with others via his teaching methods make Rob the complete package!"

— **Dan Spence, Owner, 360 Goaltending**

"Dr. Rob Graham has been a huge inspiration to everyone he meets, myself included. He brings an unbridled passion for helping and teaching others that is matched not only by his enthusiasm, but also his knowledge of teaching and learning principles. Through his engaging personality, Dr. Graham demonstrates a unique, professional, and creative approach in teaching students that reaches everyone involved. He is truly inspirational, a great mentor and he is always willing to go above and beyond to ensure he makes a positive difference to the lives he touches."

— **Doug Sanders, Top Shelf Athletics**

About the Author

Dr. Rob Graham

Techno-Resiliency™ founder and esteemed author Dr. Rob Graham empowers business and educational leaders to thrive in technology-enhanced workplaces. While earning his PhD in e-Research and technology-enhanced learning from the esteemed Lancaster University in the UK, Dr. Rob developed an award-winning, research-based theoretical lens. To date, his teachings and principles have led to global interest and the sale of thousands of copies of his Springer-published book, *Techno-Resiliency in Education*.

As a former assistant professor in the Faculty of Education of Nipissing University and an information technology and special education teacher in the public school system, Dr. Rob brings the highest level of experience to his innovative work in Techno-Resiliency™. His approach to educating and supporting organizations and academic communities is steeped in practical, lived experience and spun into an impassioned, energetic delivery. As one witnesses his actions to enable organizational and community capacity for those with a personal and professional Mandate to Be Great, it becomes clear why Dr. Rob is the "Techno-Resiliency™ Titan."

Made in the USA
Columbia, SC
01 July 2021

41109989R00095